NINE MONTHS AT GROUND ZERO

The Story of the Brotherhood of Workers
Who Took on a Job Like No Other

**Glenn Stout,
Charles Vitchers,
and Robert Gray**

SCRIBNER

New York London Toronto Sydney

SCRIBNER
1230 Avenue of the Americas
New York, NY 10020

DESIGNED BY ERICH HOBBING

Text set in Berthold Garamond

For information about special discounts for bulk purchases,
please contact Simon & Schuster Special Sales at
1-800-456-6798 or business@simonandschuster.com

Manufactured in the United States of America

10 9 8 7 6 5 4 3 2 1

Library of Congress Cataloging-in-Publication Data is available.

ISBN-13: 978-0-7432-7040-3
ISBN-10: 0-7432-7040-1

In memory of those who lost their lives on September 11,
and to their families

I dream'd in a dream, I saw a city invincible to the attacks
    of the whole of the rest of the earth;
I dream'd that was the new City of Friends;
Nothing was greater there than the quality of robust love—it led the rest;
It was seen every hour in the actions of the men of that city,
And in all their looks and words.

—WALT WHITMAN, *Leaves of Grass*

CONTENTS

NINE MONTHS
AT GROUND ZERO

PROLOGUE

To Charlie Vitchers, Bobby Gray, and the other construction workers in New York, the attack on the World Trade Center was a sucker punch to the gut. Every construction worker in the city knew someone who had worked on the Towers at one time or another—a neighbor or cousin, coworker or friend. Indeed, many had worked there themselves.

The Twin Towers were the signature buildings of New York City's construction industry—the epitome of what it could create. During the course of their construction, which began in 1966, thousands of union tradesmen had labored on the site. Their success sparked a new era in high-rise construction. In a city that hadn't seen its skyline change dramatically for years, the building of the Towers launched a construction renaissance as skyscraper after skyscraper slowly rose toward the sky. Towering monoliths crowned with strange birdlike cranes began casting their shadows across the island of Manhattan. During the next few decades, the city would take on an entirely new silhouette.

The Towers themselves were so enormous that their construction inspired logistical innovations never before used in New York City construction. Each of the 200,000 steel columns and joists were fabricated off-site and trucked in. The beams were lifted into place by cranes—built in Australia—known as kangaroos or climbing cranes. Attached to a tower fixed to the structure,

1

these cranes were jacked up and rose with the building, floor after floor.

The construction workers who built the Towers wore the experience as a badge of honor: they had built the biggest and the best. In every way this was a monumental accomplishment: they created the buildings that became a symbol of America's might and power in the world. Perhaps even more significant, the Twin Towers *were* New York. They were big and loud and brash. They had an in-your-face, take-no-prisoners attitude. And they were instantly recognizable.

While they were reviled by architects and architecture critics the world over, they quickly became the pride of New Yorkers—especially New York construction workers. Since first breaching the skyline, the Twin Towers became the touchstone against which all other jobs were compared in scale and complexity.

And when they were attacked, the response of New York's construction community was instantaneous. Before anyone articulated the need for their skills, thousands of ironworkers, crane operators, electricians, carpenters, welders, and laborers dropped what they were doing, left their work sites, and headed to Ground Zero.

Such a response was simple and uncomplicated. It was their city. Those were their buildings. From a pile of rubble so immense that it resisted description, they would restore order.

CHARLIE VITCHERS

My name is Charlie Vitchers. During the fall of 2001, I was working as a general superintendent for Bovis Lend Lease, a construction management firm.

My first real job was as a carpenter's helper, when I was fourteen. I was working off the books for, like, $3 an hour. I learned how to carry shingles, carry wood, unload trucks. Slowly, I was allowed to start nailing stuff together.

I got a real good, general jack-of-all-trades knowledge. I did some landscaping. I worked as a maintenance guy. I learned to operate road graders, backhoes, dump trucks. I was always tinkering around. I loved the fact I could work with my hands, read a blueprint. If you gave me a project, I'd get it done. This was all when I was very young, in my teens, still going to school. I was making decent money. I'd go out with my friends and I'd be the only one with a couple of bucks in my pocket. Girls loved it, too, you know?

I graduated high school in 1976, the bicentennial year, and went to work. My first wife, Marianne, and I got married a year later and we raised a very fast family, six kids in eleven years. In about 1978 my brother-in-law offered me a position as a carpenter in Manhattan if I was willing to make the commute. I paid the union initiation fee and was in the door. I went from making $8 an hour to $19.50.

I'll never forget it. On my first day of work, I was told, "Go down to the loading dock. We're bringing in Sheetrock."

I'm thinking, "What do we have? A couple of hundred boards?"

No, they had fifteen tractor trailers with 800 boards each backed up down the road. Welcome to New York City.

After a couple of weeks, they asked if I could read blueprints. I said yeah. I hardly ever unloaded a piece of Sheetrock again, and I became a foreman for that company very quickly.

There are three things I shoot for when I take on a project. One, I want the client satisfied. Two, I want to bring the job in on time. And three, I want an incident- and injury-free project. I'm not going to get someone killed on the job. The last thing I want to do is call some guy's family and try to explain why he's dead; why we didn't have safety netting in place; why we were working too fast to really care. There's always an excuse when someone gets killed, but the key is that it always could have been prevented.

Most construction people like me—managers and superintendents—have to understand every phase of a construction site. I have to know what every foreman and every tradesman knows. If a carpenter is having a problem, I have to know what he's doing and I have to know ways to do things he hasn't even thought of.

I can drive a truck. I can operate a crane. I've got thirty years in the business. I can personally jump into any trade in New York City, any trade worldwide, and produce a quality finished product because I've done so many different jobs.

I was thinking about getting out of New York construction, because what I like to do is fish. I was going to open up my own small sporting goods shop in Pennsylvania. I wanted a place where people could come and ask what flies are hatching and bullshit about fishing.

I even found a place. I was just about ready to start ordering inventory, poles and stuff like that. I planned on being open in April of 2002, opening day of trout season.

Then 9/11 happened.

CHAPTER ONE

THE ATTACKS

It is a story now heartbreakingly familiar.

An invigorating September morning, crisp and blue and perfect. New Yorkers across the city were sitting down with the Daily News *or the* Post, *making breakfast for their kids, returning from their jog, grabbing a cup of coffee, getting ready for the day ahead. Some were already on their way to the subway. And at least one particular group of New Yorkers was already at work.*

Construction workers start their days early. On the morning of September 11, 2001, the building site at the corner of 59th Street and 6th Avenue was already in full swing. The old St. Moritz Hotel was getting a full makeover.

It was an interesting job, a meticulous job. The exterior of the St. Moritz—a landmark building—was made of carved terra-cotta and decorated with gargoyles and rams' heads. All of the ornamental stone work was being taken down, piece by piece, and reset by stonemason subcontractors. The upper floors were completely enclosed by scaffolding. At the top of the building, the crew was putting up ornate brickwork on the exterior of the edifice that housed the cedar water tower. It was the last of the architectural façade work to be laid back onto the building. On the interior, renovation and rebuilding were under way on every floor.

One of the half-dozen supervisors on the site was Charlie Vitchers. A native New Yorker, Vitchers had worked construction for thirty years and was now a superintendent for Bovis Lend Lease, one of the world's largest construction management firms.

At 8:45 A.M. on that peerless September morning, with a cup of coffee in his hand, Charlie Vitchers was a content man. Three of his kids were grown and out of the house. The other three were still in school, living with their mother on Long Island. It was a beautiful fall day, the kind that makes New Yorkers fall in love with their city all over again. And while he was looking forward to opening his own bait and tackle shop, the building in which he now stood was coming along nicely, and the stone work truly was exceptional.

One minute later, at 8:46 A.M., American Airlines Flight 11 smashed into the World Trade Center Number One, the North Tower, and for Charlie Vitchers—and everyone else in the city, indeed, for all Americans— life changed forever.

CHARLIE VITCHERS

I was working on a thirty-seven-story project. From the ground up to the twenty-second floor, the St. Moritz was going to remain a hotel, but from the twenty-third floor up it was going to be residential condominiums. The building had deteriorated over the years and we were taking the top off—the twenty-eighth floor up to the thirty-seventh floor had to be removed, demolished, and rebuilt. From the twenty-second floor down, we were doing a complete gut, taking out all the walls and rebuilding each floor.

Work starts at 7 A.M., so I'd normally take the E train from my apartment in Chelsea and get there between 6 and 7. I rolled in that morning at about 7 o'clock, grabbed coffee, and did my normal routine. It was a typical day.

I got into the Alimak, an exterior hoist on the building similar to an elevator, and had coffee with the hoist operator, a guy named Smitty. He brought me all the way up to the roof. I generally start each day on the job with a safety walk-through. It's the superintendent's responsibility to make a quick run-through of the building to make a safety assessment, to make sure that all the nets and other safety systems are in place, and if they're not, to report by radio to whoever's responsible for the safety of the job. You have to make sure that all the safety rules spelled out in Article 19 of the New York building code are followed.

I started at the top and walked down. You hit every floor where guys are working. At about the twenty-fifth or twenty-sixth floor, just before 9 A.M., Smitty came back up on the hoist and said, "A plane just crashed into the World Trade Center."

I said, "What kind of plane?"

"I don't know," he said. "We just heard it on the news."

We went up to the roof but didn't have a view of the World Trade Center from that building. We even climbed up on the ladder on the outside of the water tower to get another twenty feet higher. But we still couldn't see the Trade Center. We were blocked by most of the tall buildings in and around Times Square. We couldn't see anything downtown at first, no smoke, nothing.

Some of the guys had a radio and heard reports that a plane hit the building. A lot of guys, including myself, were thinking it must have been a student pilot that flew out of Teterboro. A freak thing.

Then we started to see smoke above the skyline. Now I'm thinking, "Holy shit. That must be a major fire." Then I saw this flash, a bright orange fireball explode out to the east. It created a plume of smoke that shot straight out horizontally and then just disappeared. I figured the plane that had hit the building had blown up.

Then I got word from someone that a second plane had hit the second tower. At that point, I knew something was up. I got a call on the cell phone from Jon Kraft, the general super on the job. At Bovis, the general superintendent is a formal title for the super in charge of a project worth over $60 million or more than a million square feet, and this job was that big. I was a superintendent working under the general super.

He said, "Charlie, we're evacuating the building. Something's going on downtown." I called my foremen and told them to tell everyone to leave, then I walked from the top down to make sure everyone was gone. I walked all the floors, went into all the mechanical rooms, went into all the machine rooms and checked, just in case there was a guy in there listening to headphones while he's screwing a motor together or something. I found a couple of steamfitters having coffee and told them to get out.

I still didn't really know what was going on. I walked down the stairs, went into the operator's shanty. In there were about twenty-five guys all staring at a television watching the second plane go into the South Tower.

Just south of Charlie Vitchers's work site, another man was watching the same scene. His name was Bobby Gray.

Gray is an operating engineer, a crane operator. So is his older brother. So is his younger brother. His father was an operating engineer, as well. It's a tradition; it's in the blood.

On September 11, 2001, Bobby Gray was perched in a crane fifty stories up, at a building site on the edge of Times Square. A member of Local 14 of the International Union of Operating Engineers, Gray is certified to operate virtually all heavy machinery, though for the last twenty years he has worked almost exclusively on the behemoth machines known as climbing cranes. He is a second-generation New Yorker. His father was born in Hell's Kitchen and raised his family in Yonkers.

Construction is a sophisticated business. The level of complexity involved in raising a seventy-story superstructure is staggering. One of the most important—and nerve-racking—jobs on a skyscraper build is that of crane operator. Gray will tell you it's also the most fun. After all, Bobby Gray quit college because he felt more comfortable sitting on a piece of heavy machinery than sitting in anatomy class.

Working with ironworkers, Bobby, as operating engineer, must ensure that each steel beam—and all other material too big or too heavy to go in the hoist—is raised safely to the top of the building and then set precisely into place. When the job is done well, no one notices—a building rises slowly on the horizon. When it is not, it becomes a headline. There is no margin for error; errors get people killed.

At 8:45 A.M. that morning, as he maneuvered a bucket full of 3½ cubic yards of concrete 600 feet in the air, a streak across the sky broke Gray's concentration.

BOBBY GRAY

On September 11, I was working just west of Times Square on 43rd Street and 8th Avenue, across the street from *The New York Times* building. The crane was at the top of the building, fifty stories, 500 or 600 feet, off the ground, what we call topped out, meaning we weren't adding any more floors. The crane always sits higher than the building so the crane deck can swing around 360 degrees without obstruction. The boom of the crane reached up another couple of hundred feet.

The night before there was a Monday night football game. I remember having maybe one beer too many and waking up a little bit later than I should have. I was supposed to be in the crane for a 6 o'clock start and I was running late.

Going to work I remember thinking it was going to be a great sunrise—the sun came up at about 6:30 A.M. I usually wear boat shoes and shorts to work and then change, put my work shoes on, and climb up the crane. The morning of September 11, I didn't have time to do that. I climbed the crane wearing a pair of deck shoes, a pair of shorts, a T-shirt, and a sweat shirt. It was my favorite weather. It was cool, kind of crisp, not a cloud in the sky. My younger brother, Michael, was also on a climber crane, maybe fifteen, twenty blocks away. I could see his crane clear as a bell.

Then about 8:45 A.M. a jet flew over. I was like, "WOW! Holy shit, this guy is low! What's he doing so low?" I had *never* seen a plane that low in Manhattan.

I was lifting up a bucketful of concrete to pour a floor deck and turned back to pay attention to what I was doing. Then my girlfriend called me on the cell phone and told me a plane had hit the Towers. I had a regular AM/FM radio in the cab and I started listening. I put it on the PA system so everyone on the roof deck could hear. I looked out the window of the crane downtown. I could see about half of the North Tower and just a sliver of the South Tower behind it and could see the smoke pouring out. Because of my perspective, I wasn't sure which building had been hit.

At first they were reporting it was a small plane and for a few minutes I didn't even put it together that the plane that hit the North Tower was the plane that flew right over us. Then everyone on the roof looked at each other and went, "Holy shit—that had to be the same plane."

We could all see the smoke pouring out and blowing to the east. That's when the South Tower got hit. We could only see just a little bit of it, but we actually saw this fireball blowing out of the side of the South Tower. I thought that maybe something inside the North Tower had ignited and caused the fireball, maybe the plane hit the mechanical room and it caused some kind of explosion. We didn't realize that another plane had come in from the south. And then of course that came in over the radio. And everybody was just stunned. Just absolutely stunned.

Gray's assumption was correct. The plane that passed over his head was Flight 11. After taking off from Boston at 8:00 A.M., Flight 11 was hijacked en route to Los Angeles and turned south, roughly following the Hudson River toward New York, and entered air space above northern Manhattan, far uptown. Less than forty seconds later, tracking almost due south at nearly 500 miles per hour, the 767 passed over Times Square. Twenty seconds after Gray first saw the plane, it smashed into the façade of the North Tower. The nose of the plane entered the building at the ninety-fourth floor, more than 1,000 feet above the ground, and was swallowed up in a quarter of a second. Fourteen hundred people were working above the floor of impact. None would survive.

Seventeen minutes later, at 9:03, United Airlines Flight 175 similarly violated the South Tower, World Trade Center Two. Only forty-six minutes would pass between the moment of impact and that of collapse. Approximately 8,500 people were already at work in Tower Two. Of those who worked below the point of impact, the vast majority would survive. Above the point of impact, most would perish.

The world watched with growing horror as billows of black smoke spread over downtown Manhattan. Soon flames could be seen in the furious clouds of ash. Debris and worse began to rain onto the plaza. In those early minutes, shock, paralysis, and fear gripped the country; such an abomination could not happen here.

Stunned with incomprehension, New Yorkers struggled to react.

CHARLIE VITCHERS

I stared at that TV in disbelief. At first everybody on the site was stunned; nobody knew what to do.

Port Authority was closing the bridges and tunnels. New York was shutting down. We sent home about 300 people—everybody who wasn't on our Bovis payroll, all the subcontractors, electricians, steamfitters, carpenters, plumbers, and masons. The only people that stayed were a couple operating engineers we needed to run the hoists and our own staff of supervisors and laborers. Maybe a couple dozen people. The general super sent the whole project team into the main office on the third floor. Jim Abadie, a VP with Bovis, was going to get back to us at 1 o'clock to let us know who was staying and who could go home.

Every fire truck . . . every police car was blowing like thunder downtown. The streets were just loaded with people walking. Hundreds of thousands of people not saying hardly a word, all heading in the same direction, all just getting out of New York City. There was no panic. People were just walking away.

When I first saw the footage of the Towers on fire on TV, I didn't know those buildings were going to come down. I thought the sprinkler system might extinguish the flames. But after seeing that fireball and knowing the construction of those buildings, there was no doubt in my mind that if the floors above started to collapse—they would be the first ones to go because of the heat—they would just drop down on top of each other. If every floor above the fire suddenly collapsed, there was no way that building was going to sustain the weight of all those floors collapsing from above.

BOBBY GRAY

I climbed down from the crane and walked up 43rd Street into Times Square. They had a shot of the Towers on the big Jumbotron television and I saw the South Tower fall. Even with all my experience in construction, I never, never ever, *never ever* imagined it was going to fall.

Some people were still going about their business—I don't know if they didn't know what had happened or what. I remember thinking of the casualties and almost not being able to breathe. Just to see it, the way it came down, knowing that place, having been there, having worked down there, I thought we had just lost 60,000 people.

I was like most New Yorkers; the Trade Center was a place you knew. I worked Seven World Trade Center when it was being built, and then I worked on it for months and months and months on a rehab, which is when you refit floors or portions of a building for a new client, or have to lift and install new mechanical systems. I knew the underground PATH station and the shopping malls underneath there. When I worked in Battery Park City we used to go to a bar after work on the forty-fourth floor of one of the Towers. It was great because you could look out the window and see the job you were working on.

That's why I was thinking the number of casualties was going to be catastrophic, horrific. Core columns are denser and heavier and more robust than exterior columns because they carry the load of the building. I've worked with single columns that weighed more than 90 tons. There were massive, massive columns in the Towers and the destruction they would cause in a collapse would be horrible, which turned out to be true. They were rectangular, maybe four foot by a foot and a half, about two stories tall, and weighed 60 tons each. And there were hundreds of them.

I walked back from Times Square. By this time the job was pretty much shut down. I grabbed my partner, Hughie Manley, and another guy, Dutch, and another engineer named Jerry. We all laced up and said, "We're going downtown."

I wasn't thinking about running cranes down there yet. I just knew they were going to need help, period. Especially once the North Tower collapsed.

Once we started to walk downtown, we passed a building that had a cherry picker out front—a small mobile crane. One of the guys said, "Let's hot-wire it." I went up to a cop and asked, "Do you mind if we steal it and take it downtown?"

He told us to go ahead, but then the contractor showed up and freaked out so we just kept walking. Down in Greenwich Village somewhere, I said, "Look, we better get something to eat because once we go in . . . There's nothing there anymore."

I've always been laid back. I never tell anybody what to do or anything like that. But while we were sitting at this pizza place I said to every guy with me, "You really better think about whether you want to go in or not. You're going to see things you're going to remember the rest of your life."

I don't know what compelled me to go, but I knew that I had to. I just wanted to help.

It was a time of such chaos and indecision. I was single and didn't have a family to worry about. My girlfriend Jo-Ann was in South Jersey and I couldn't get there anyway. All I knew was that I had to go there and damned if I wasn't. The cops weren't going to stop me; no one was going to stop me.

CHARLIE VITCHERS

All of the people that I was with had already made up our minds: we were going downtown. But we were told to go back over to the St. Moritz and hang out and wait to hear from our boss at Bovis, Jim Abadie.

About 1 o'clock Abadie called. Bovis was already working on a hotel near the Trade Center in Battery Park City, doing the final fit outs and finish work, getting ready for the grand opening in just a couple of weeks. Abadie wanted to know who was willing to go down to the Trade Center and help out. He said there was a bus for Bovis leaving from the Javits Center over by the Lincoln Tunnel, and for us to get down there, look for the group of Bovis guys, and then just follow whatever directions.

I just grabbed my knapsack and said, "I'm ready, man. I'm out of here."

I walked over to the Javits Center but there was no bus. Nothing was set up yet. But everybody there was like "one for all, all for one," and started walking downtown, either individually or with whatever group of guys they came with.

I walked down West Street toward the Trade Center but the Military Police stopped me. They said, "You can't go this way."

I go, "I'm with Bovis, I have my hardhat."

They said, "We don't care who you're with, you're not going any farther."

So I said, okay, and started heading east where I ran into more MPs. By about 5 o'clock, I was about a quarter mile away from the Trade Center. I had a clear view down Washington Street of Building Seven, which was on the north edge of the site. All forty-seven stories were on fire. It was wild. The MPs said the building was going to collapse. I said, "Nah, I don't know." And then all of a sudden I watched the building shake like an earthquake hit it, and the building came down.

And I just said, "Holy shit."

The MPs that had been there were no longer there. The demarcation line that was set up was gone. So I kept walking.

I saw a guy with a Bovis hat that I didn't know and he told me, "We're supposed to meet here, we're waiting for Jim Abadie." By now, it's around 7 o'clock. It was starting to get dark. I had spent six hours just walking the streets.

Finally someone came down with Bovis letterhead stationery and cut out the letterhead, put it in a little plastic I.D. tag, passed them out and told us the Bovis trailer was set up at One World Financial Center, on the southwest corner of the site.

"Try and get down there," was what they told us.

All morning, all through the afternoon and into the evening, virtually the entire population of lower Manhattan streamed silently away from the Trade Center. Thousands of New Yorkers trudged northward, glancing back nervously to stare in disbelief at the growing cloud of smoke hanging over the city, wondering if there were still more attacks to come. The rest of the nation—indeed much of the world—huddled before their televisions, as coverage of the carnage looped again and again and again.

Thousands, however, made their way in the opposite direction, pushing against the tide, dodging the hastily assembled security cordon. They were firemen and policemen, emergency services personnel, construction workers. And there were hundreds, perhaps thousands, of average citizens, driven by an innate need to do something, anything. To respond.

What they found was devastation beyond comprehension. It was bedlam.

BOBBY GRAY

Up around Greenwich Street, north of Chambers it was a mess. There were probably thousands of people there. You could hardly see. There was paper and dust on the streets, all the fallout from the collapse of the Towers.

At the corner of Chambers and West Street, about a quarter mile north of the North Tower, the FDNY had set up a temporary command station under the pedestrian bridges—just a couple of fire trucks and some FDNY commanders. They were wearing white shirts and were surrounded by firefighters, so I knew they were in a position of authority. Down by the Trade Center, I could even see some columns from the Towers impaled in the ground.

There was more chaos than control. People were frantic, but except for the fire radios, I remember it being pretty quiet. Firefighters were walking into the area from the Trade Center, covered with dust.

I spotted Mike Marrone from Bovis Lend Lease. He had been the general super when I had worked on the Trump Tower, the tallest residential building in the world. He saw me and said, "Stick around. I'm going to need you."

Suddenly we saw firemen running and yelling, "Seven's going to go, seven's going to go!" Seconds later, Building Seven is gone.

I watched the southeast corner of the roof kind of buckle and then the building came straight down. Clouds of dust rolled and blew down the side streets like a hurricane going horizontally. A lot of people ran. I couldn't. I was standing on the street about two blocks away, frozen.

CHARLIE VITCHERS

When I finally got to the Trade Center my initial reaction was to see if I could find anybody alive. But instead I did my own walk-around assessment and went completely around the whole site. I couldn't find Albany Street, where the Bovis trailer was. Nothing looked the same. I didn't recognize anything south of Vesey Street. The bridge over West Street that connected the World Financial Center to the Trade Center was down. Steel columns—what we call "sticks"—from Tower One were impaled right in the middle of West Street, sticking 60 feet up out of the ground. Nothing was recognizable. Everything was just one big pile of debris and there was almost no ambient light, just a little from some emergency lights in buildings around the site and from police and fire vehicles on the perimeter. You couldn't even tell where the open plaza was that had been between the two Towers. It just didn't really seem real. I just walked around and said, "Where the hell am I?"

Firemen were already up on the pile. There were thousands of people there, bucket brigades with a couple hundred people in them snaking all over the place.

I tried to find Albany Street because I knew where the 1010 Firehouse was from working down there. But I couldn't find it. I mean it was there, but I couldn't find it. On Liberty Street I saw a taxi cab completely covered with debris, impaled with stone and steel from the Tower. Half of the front was crushed into the debris pile. The rear end of the taxi was sticking up in the air and the left tail light was blinking.

And the smoke. You couldn't see your hand in front of your face. The wind would blow and all of a sudden you'd be in a cloud of dust and smoke, you'd have to stop and crouch down low to figure out where the hell you were walking.

When night fell, it was totally disorienting, eerie. It was like looking at downtown Manhattan in a blackout.

There were no streetlights.

There was nothing.

CHAPTER TWO

RESPONSE

The degree of destruction was mind-boggling in scale and complexity. When they fell, the buildings were broken into their component parts in a tangle of debris, much of it burning and exhaling dense clouds of smoke. From the two Towers alone, 400 million pounds of steel columns, trusses, and reinforcing bars were turned to twisted scrap. Six hundred thousand square feet of thick window glass was shattered. The detritus of American corporate life—chairs, desks, files, and computers—vanished along with those who worked there.

Though jagged portions of the Towers' façades loomed twenty stories in the air, the immense mass of rubble caused many first responders to pause and stare in disbelief. It simply did not seem possible that two of the world's largest buildings had all but disappeared.

And they had, at least partially. The wreckage extended as much as seventy feet below grade, through six basement levels to the bedrock foundations that had once supported two of the tallest buildings in the world. In total, 2,700 vertical feet of building, containing nearly 10 million square feet of floor space, were reduced to a tangled, smoking, burning heap less than 200 feet thick. It spilled beyond the sixteen-acre parcel of the Trade Center complex to encompass an area more than twice that size. The debris field was contained only by the barricade of the surrounding buildings, many of which were now more rubble than structure.

Debris from the North Tower had punched a hole completely through the eight-story U.S. Customs House. Nearly thirty stories above the ground, columns from the North Tower pierced the American Express Building. The fall of the South Tower obliterated the tiny, two-story St. Nicholas Greek Orthodox Church tucked beneath it on Liberty Street and flattened all but the bottom few floors of the twenty-two-story Vista Marriott Hotel, which sat in its shadow due west.

Virtually every surrounding building suffered significant harm. Façades facing the Trade Center were sandblasted by debris. Windows and doors blew out. Ninety West Street—a half block south—was in flames.

But none of this mattered. The destruction of the buildings was not what drew Charlie Vitchers and Bobby Gray and Jim Abadie to the burning rubble of Ground Zero. It wasn't what kept the FDNY at the top of the pile around the clock, nor was it what riveted the world on that September day. What mattered now was the possibility that people might still be alive, that there might be survivors. From the wreckage, the clock began to tick. Finding survivors became a frantic, desperate race.

Starting at the fringes, rescuers were already moving over the ruins. Wherever conditions allowed, they climbed in and over and under the rubble. Where they encountered loose rubble, they dug with their hands or used smaller pieces of debris—lengths of rebar, hooks of splintered steel, shards of concrete—to pry up larger pieces of wreckage. Some used picks and axes liberated from crushed fire and rescue vehicles. Bucket brigades made up of dozens and dozens of people spontaneously formed, snaking along hundreds of feet. They were looking for voids, cavelike air pockets under the debris. Only in those voids, they reasoned, would survivors be found. When they did uncover one, rescuers crawled in, calling for survivors, shining flashlights, feeling their way with their hands.

The pile was probed this way in hundreds of places at once, each individual operation an ad hoc response. The scene was frantic and desperate, yet it was not rushed, for the pile itself was such a formidable obstacle that moving quickly over it was virtually impossible. The rubble was still shifting, making each step perilous. And everywhere, the path was blocked by enormous steel beams.

MICHAEL BANKER, FDNY

I remember towards the end of the first day being totally shot. Guys were looking for somebody to take control. I spread my guys out so if anything happened we wouldn't lose too many men all at once.

We were totally done. I mean, we were dead in the water, man. Then all of a sudden machinery started coming in from behind Battery Park behind West Street towards the water. Frontend loaders, backhoes, cranes.

I said to one guy, "Where'd you come from, who are you?"

He says, "We were on the Williamsburg Bridge and my boss seen it happen on TV. He called up the job site and says get everything we got down here."

You talk about construction workers . . .

There was no precedent for the level of response to the tragedy. When the Towers fell, thousands of ironworkers, carpenters, crane operators, laborers, and welders mobilized. Assessing the on-site needs from the television images they were seeing, foremen and supervisors picked up the phone and began to muster workers and machinery.

What they recognized was that without massive logistical and mechanical support, the firemen, policemen, and volunteer bucket brigades digging through ash and rubble with their bare hands would be able to move only an infinitesimal amount of the debris.

Had this been a "normal" disaster, the governmental agencies already in place to deal with emergencies—such as the mayor's Office of Emergency Management, FEMA, the Federal Office of Emergency Management, or the U.S. Army Corps of Engineers—would have taken over. But Building Seven, which had burned and collapsed, housed the command center of the mayor's Office of Emergency Management. The agency occupied the entire twenty-third floor in a secure, self-contained emergency bunker—with its own fuel supply, generators, food, water, and communications systems—designed to allow the city to continue to govern and coordinate emergency response and recovery efforts. From the bunker, city officials had envisioned contacting other governmental agencies and coordinating police, fire, and other emergency responders if some horrific event made it impossible to do so from City Hall or any other civic building. But the destruction of the bunker itself had never been envisioned. Its annihilation, coupled with the near total loss of communication and electricity in lower Manhattan, created a void of truly monumental proportions.

In the initial confusion, as civilian construction crews swung into action, New York City's Department of Design and Construction (DDC)—a city agency charged with overseeing the building and maintenance of the city's infrastructure, such as schools, water lines, and sidewalks—assumed first authority over the site.

Purely by chance, several key members of the DDC, including commissioner Ken Holden and deputy commissioner Michael Burton, were on their way to a meeting at City Hall when the Towers were struck. DDC agency heads knew the major players in New York construction and knew those companies had the equipment, expertise, and manpower needed to address the immediate needs at the site.

One of the first people they called was forty-four-year-old Jim Abadie.

Abadie was senior vice president in charge of operations for the New York office of Bovis Lend Lease, one of the largest construction management firms in the world. Even before the DDC could track him down, Abadie knew the disaster at the World Trade Center was on a scale beyond the capability of any single agency or group. His firm's experience and expertise would be needed; so too would others'. A native of Queens, Abadie had spent his high school and college summers working as a laborer. After graduating in 1981 from Syracuse University with a degree in civil engineering, he went to work with the construction company Lehr McGovern, which was eventually taken over by Bovis Lend Lease.

JIM ABADIE, BOVIS

I've done a lot of projects in New York over the years. I've worked on the American Stock Exchange, the Bank of America, *The New York Times*. On September 11, I was in charge of all the superintendents, laborers, and on-site project activities that emanated from the New York office. That morning I left my senior staff meeting a little early. My phone rings. It was one of my superintendents at the job we had at the tip of Battery Park City, at the Ritz-Carlton Hotel.

He said, "Jim, I just want to let you know there's a massive fire going on in the North Tower down at the Trade Center."

"Okay," I said. "Keep me posted." Then he called me again from the roof of the Ritz-Carlton and starts screaming on the phone, "A plane just went over my head and hit the South Tower!"

I knew then there were serious, serious issues. Later that morning I got a phone call from Lou Mendes, assistant deputy commissioner of the DDC. Bovis had done a lot of work for the DDC. In 1998, a piece of concrete fell from the ceiling at Yankee Stadium onto the seats. We got called in and worked around the clock for seven days to put protection in there, so I had gotten to know the guys from the DDC and the Office of Emergency Management (OEM) pretty well.

Mendes asked, "Can you help? We're going to try to get a couple more construction-type people in and we'll get a police van and get you down there."

"Sure," I said, "I'll help."

At 12 o'clock a police van came and picked me up. Richard Tomasetti, an engineer, was already in the van and I had one of my superintendents with me, Mike Marrone. We were only able to get to Intermediate School 89 (IS 89), at Chambers and West Street, a quarter mile north of the site, which had been commandeered as a command center. Then we started walking. The closer we got to the site, it looked like it had snowed.

We started doing a walk-around. I could go on for hours on what the disaster looked like, all the people trying to go on the pile to get at stuff. We went down Albany Street and I remember looking down and seeing a tire from one of the airplanes, a whole tire and assembly that had blown off one of the planes, two blocks away from the Trade Center.

We went to One Police Plaza and the DDC asked us, "What do you think you guys can do?" I said, "We gotta start calling crane companies, we gotta start calling equipment companies and start getting this thing geared up. We've got to be able to get to the site." I had Mike call some of our supers in, and I already had people at the Battery Park City job. Every time I got ahold of a contractor with a piece of equipment, the DDC arranged for police escorts. They all started coming.

There was no contract, and no talk about contracts. It was just, "Get equipment here. We have to help."

No matter who I got ahold of, nobody said no. Everybody wanted to do more.

BOBBY GRAY

Mike Marrone asked me to go to a meeting at One Police Plaza, headquarters of the New York City Police Department, about five or six blocks east of the Trade Center near City Hall. We had to walk over debris. Dust was everywhere. It was like walking on the moon. Sanitation trucks had their headlights on and were trying to get over to the site. It made everything look like a blizzard. There was no power, no electricity. And this was probably four or five blocks north of the actual Ground Zero site. At One Police Plaza we went through a security check and into a room on the second floor. Some of the biggest contractors in the city were there. No phones in the building were working.

I'm saying to myself, "This is One Police Plaza, police headquarters, and there's not a working phone. I can't believe it."

The meeting at One Police Plaza was the first stirring of a collaboration that was to last for nine months and evolve into one of the biggest demo jobs of all time. But before that, before anything else, the search for survivors took priority. The men in that conference room knew with great certainty that the problem was the pile. They had to get onto the pile, where, only blocks away, with little coordination and virtually no communication, a massive search and rescue operation had begun.

CHARLIE VITCHERS

When I finally got to Albany Street, to the Bovis trailer, on the southwest corner of the site, they were bringing in equipment.

There was all kinds of stuff just rolling in, some by truck, some by barge to nearby piers. We were trying to get ahold of electricians to set up lights and get ourselves situated. We already had a team of guys down there, and pulled some generators off the Bovis job site and were working off of the street.

At One World Financial—the AmEx Building—the loading dock was open; when the power went out they couldn't shut the gate. We talked to the building superintendent, and said, "Look, we're Bovis Lend Lease, we're setting up, do you mind if we move in?" Their guy said, "No problem at all." So we commandeered the loading dock.

It was empty. There were no trucks parked in there; it was a tremendous area with lots of space, a high ceiling, open to the street but still protected overhead. We set up shop there and Bovis moved a trailer up from Battery Park. Jimmy Lomma, who owned Lomma Crane & Rigging, brought in by barge a mobile home, one of those drive-across-the-country things, because we knew some guys were going to be sleeping there around the clock.

Bovis had probably about fifteen to twenty laborers and there were probably ten superintendents originally assigned to leave their other jobs and meet there. I had been told to speak with Nick Bruzzese, one of our superintendents. When I got down there I walked up to him and said, "I'm Charlie Vitchers."

Nick says, "Charlie, just go out there and do whatever it is that you do best . . . What is it that you do best?"

I says, "I do anything, Nick."

"Look, we don't have an assignment for you right now. Just go out there and report back here. We're going to have a meeting again at nine o'clock."

I was like, "Okay." So I went out.

I figured if I had any expertise to add down there it would be in some kind of logistics, maybe just moving trucks around or running a certain crew of people, anything. The firemen were trying to get hoses out onto the pile. I helped them with the hoses. We had guys that were trying to move cars out of the way so we could clear West Street, so I commandeered one of the guys who was driving a forklift and another guy who was on a frontend loader.

I said, "Hook up these cars and take them all the way down West Street. Take them down to the Battery Tunnel and just start stockpiling cars down there. If it ain't on fire, pick it up and move it. Let's clear off West Street."

That's basically the first thing we did. We just needed to get access into the site. There were fire trucks that were crushed, that were on fire, that were collapsed. We picked them up. We moved anything we could find and tried to find a place where it wouldn't be in the way so we could get closer into the site. The firemen needed to get into that pile to look for survivors. That was the game plan.

We had ironworkers out on the pile who didn't have oxygen hoses for their torches long enough to reach inside the pile, so they could cut steel and move it to look for people. All sorts of supplies were already coming in by boat to one of the piers. We found crates and crates of extra hoses, but didn't have the male/female couplers to tie the hoses together. I went to the pier and started rummaging around, tearing open boxes, and finally found cases and cases and cases of connectors. I stuffed my pockets with them and I came back out to the site and I started handing them to the ironworkers. Now their forty-foot hoses became two-hundred-foot hoses. It got them a lot farther out onto the pile.

There was no coordination yet. The fire department had had hoses on 90 West Street for a while, then took them off when they thought they'd extinguished it, thinking it was under control. A couple of times, I would notice flames coming out of the third floor. I'd go grab one of the fire department guys and say, "Hey, this building's on fire again." They'd find a guy with a water truck, and get him over there, and they'd spray it down again. That building burned for forty-eight hours until they finally got it under control. It was pretty chaotic. Everybody was doing what they could do based on common sense.

BOBBY GRAY

I was at One Police Plaza throwing out ideas of how we were going to initiate the response from the construction end of it, what kind of equipment we were going to try and get in and so on and so forth. It was mostly senior VPs from the construction industry, maybe even a president or so. AMEC was in there, Tully was represented, Bovis was in there, mostly high-end people from the big contractors, ten, maybe twelve people. That was the first time I'd met Mike Burton of the DDC, who eventually ran the job for the DDC, along with Ken Holden.

Only one person had a working cell phone. I took it and started calling vendors and trying to get operators. I guess I was the crane guy then, the Master Mechanic. But I really wasn't thinking that way. I just started calling. I knew where a couple of the bigger cranes were, and at that point we were looking for big capacity hydraulic cranes. From my experience I thought we would need these big cranes because I didn't know what else we were going to be able to start with. At that point I hadn't gotten onto the pile. All I had seen was the periphery.

It was dark when we came out of the meeting. They put most of us in a big van and we went back down to the site. We parked on West Street and walked north, up to somewhere around Albany Street. That's where the real pile began. It was chaotic. But there was something about it that was just incredibly moving, to see the response of so many people. But I also knew that it was incredibly, incredibly dangerous. It made you feel good to see it, but you also knew it couldn't go on . . . there was no control. This was not going to work this way. I was looking at something I really thought we were going to take years doing.

I remember feeling so empty. I wasn't shocked. I wasn't sad. I wasn't angry. I wasn't thinking revenge. I was just . . . I don't know how to describe it. I was just empty. Just to look at this thing and forget about trying to think that it was downtown Manhattan. Just looking at it. I didn't think anything. I just couldn't comprehend what I was seeing.

Walking in, I saw my first body part. An arm and a hand sticking up. I knew it was a woman. I must have stood there for fifteen minutes. I didn't know what to do. I was frozen.

Remember the Pick-up Sticks game you played as a kid? I was looking at this massive steel everywhere, like pick-up sticks. West Street did not exist anymore. The debris pile literally went right up to the east wall of Battery Park City, to the office towers there. I remember there was a fire truck, a command station that had been set up on West Street. It was crushed, four or five feet high, and we were walking on top of it.

I walked a little bit farther in, underneath the south pedestrian bridge still standing over West Street. I walked up on the steel debris. The ironworkers were already involved. They were trying to cut a fireman out from underneath some of the steel. Then I heard a voice that I recognized, a guy I had worked with years ago, an ironworker originally from Alabama. It was *so* reassuring, that one of the first people I encountered was someone I had worked with. I was like, "Oh, man. Randy. You know what? We're going to do this. We are going to do this."

We kind of hugged and he just went right back to work. I don't think I ever saw him on the site again.

• • •

Ironworkers from Local 40 of New York were one of the first groups of construction workers to arrive on-site. They, perhaps even more than any other union, were bound to the Trade Center, for the Towers quite literally represented the high point of their industry. More than 600 ironworkers had been employed when the Towers were first built, hundreds more when the surrounding buildings went up. Several dozen members of the union who had originally worked on the Towers were still active in the union. When the buildings fell, they saw the disaster from a unique perspective—it was a steel job. They knew how the buildings had been built and they knew how the debris could be removed. Just as the steel had once been lifted by crane for the ironworkers to connect, now ironworkers would cut the steel apart, and operating engineers would move it out using cranes and other heavy equipment. No one else possessed the needed skills or experience to do so.

WILLIE QUINLAN, IRONWORKER

I couldn't believe what I was seeing and there is no way of explaining it. I thought iron was a lot stronger, but coming down that distance it just buckled and bent and twisted the way it wanted to. Bottoms of the columns were mushroomed and bent like bananas.

I could read the pile because I was there when it went up. I knew how heavy the steel was because the location and the floors and weight are engraved in a code onto the steel. It told you everything.

But it was such a mess. Everything was flattened. There were columns all over the place, columns sticking into the side of the American Express Building.

But the main thing then was to find survivors.

It was important that we got cranes in as soon as possible to start ripping everything apart, but there were already ironworkers on the pile cutting steel. We had to get the rigs together and start removing the iron from the pile because you couldn't do much more searching with all that heavy iron on top of everything.

When you run into a disaster like this, you have no plans. You've got nothing. You don't know what steel is "good" and what is "bad." You really have to look at it, because if you don't, you're gonna run into problems. If you cut something, something else is going to collapse. It was very dangerous, you were never on sure ground and there was heat and there were fires all over the place. It was hard to maneuver around.

I had worked demolition jobs before and this was a demo job. On a demo job we don't unbolt the iron or anything like that. We usually use torches to cut it apart, but at the Trade Center the iron was so heavy you couldn't cut it with just a torch. We had to use a lance, a long magnesium rod, and compressed oxygen and a torch to light it. It burns at about 7,000 degrees and will cut through anything you put in front of it, even concrete. It's just like a volcano with the lava running out.

BOBBY GRAY

I walked through the pile, up to what used to be the north pedestrian bridge, trying to figure out if we were going to be able to get anything in from the north side, the north end of West Street. That north bridge had basically collapsed. Some of the steel that had gone into those bridges was massive because they spanned the West Side Highway. A good friend of mine actually set some of the steel. "We had to walk with them," he said, which is pretty tricky. You pick the whole piece up off the ground and hold it in the air. Then you walk the machine and move the piece that way, very slowly, because you have to control momentum and you're already at capacity. If the steel starts to swing, it can pull the whole crane over. Big steel like that was collapsed right across the West Side Highway.

The area was real tricky. Four seventy-two-inch watermains, which filled the condensers with water from the Hudson, ran under West Street and zigzagged around the foundation for Battery Park City. I knew we would have to worry about that because of the weight of the cranes. But you couldn't even see where the street was.

CHARLIE VITCHERS

I knew in my heart that we were there to stay. I knew Bovis's reputation in the city and I knew our ability as a construction management team. What we had to bring to the table was valuable. The same goes for Tishman and Turner and Tully and AMEC, the other contractors, everybody.

I did not stay out that whole night. Jim Abadie finally got down to the site late that night.

"Charlie," he said. "You've been staying in the city, right? Go home. Pack some clothes and get your ass back here as soon as you can."

That was probably at about 10 o'clock that night. So I left, I put my thumb out, a cop saw my hardhat, I told him I needed a ride, and he took me uptown.

I hung out at my apartment with my girlfriend, Holly, talking about what was going on. I told her I was going to be assigned down at the site, that I was told I needed to get back down there as soon as possible. I couldn't sleep. By 2 o'clock in the morning I just couldn't sit there anymore.

I packed a knapsack and I put some clothes in there—a pair of socks, a couple of pairs of underwear, a couple of shirts—and then I went back out and I started walking downtown. I grabbed a cab, he drove me as far south as he could, and I got out and walked the rest of the way.

The guy didn't charge me.

Sometime after midnight, in the first hours of the morning of September 12, Jim Abadie sat down for a moment and began to fill out the standard, blank, one-page "Superintendent's Daily Report" covering the construction activities of the first day. For project heading he wrote "W.T.C." and dated it "9/11/01."

Below that, in neat, empty columns on the left side of the page, was space to list each contractor working under his authority on a given job, their trade, major pieces of equipment, number of employees, and the total number of hours they worked. All of that was pointless and would remain so for the next few days. There were already thousands of workers and hundreds of contractors with a presence on the site. It would be some time before such a basic level of control would come to Ground Zero. No one from the construction industry was on a payroll, making the accounting of hours meaningless. And as of that moment, technically, neither Bovis nor anyone else was supervising anyone. They were all just there, doing what seemed to make sense, responding to immediate needs.

Under the column heading "Work Performed," Abadie jotted down "4 P.M.—Mobilization," then listed a few odd pieces of heavy machinery before stopping. Recalling an event from earlier that day, he added another notation that underscored the challenge the pile presented them. He wrote,

"4 P.M. Excavator demolished by shifting materials." Beneath that, per-haps recognizing that for the moment they were all down there on their own, he wrote, *"Ironworkers, 200. (volunteers)."*

Then, as if a reminder to himself, at the bottom of the page Abadie drew an asterisk and added a final entry:

"As the steel gets removed, the fire department sorts through the debris."

CHAPTER THREE

SEPTEMBER 12, 2001

In the twenty-four hours following the attacks, men, women, and machinery streamed into lower Manhattan. By the morning of September 12, at least 5,000 people—firemen, cops, ironworkers, carpenters, office workers, financial analysts, janitors—were on-site.

Through the night, they had searched for survivors, spelunking deep into the subterranean levels, marking searched areas with spray paint, and hauling out bucket after white bucket of debris. All were spent. Most worked nonstop through the night with no thought of sleep. None had any intention of leaving.

From afar, the pile appeared alive. Fire, smoke, and steam belched from the rubble. Firemen, construction workers, policemen, and regular New Yorkers stood shoulder to shoulder, poring over the debris by hand. The air was hot and nearly windless as the heat thermals, created by the fires, pulled oxygen inward and sent black smoke nearly straight up into the sky before the prevailing wind punched through and carried it away. Surrounding streets were clogged with cranes, supply trucks, and other heavy equipment, while fire trucks nestled into every nook and cranny and poured water onto the fires that spewed out acrid smoke and white-hot flame. The dust that lay on the ground everywhere began to turn to mud as broken watermains and ambient water from fire hoses ran down the streets and clogged storm sewers. The few small trees that still stood along the perimeter bent away from the site and were nearly stripped of leaves, as if hit by a hurricane. Nearby parks, parking lots, alleyways, and other empty spaces had been commandeered for staging areas.

CHARLIE VITCHERS

On September 12, I got to the Trade Center at 4 A.M. or so. It was still dark and I walked the site again. I went by Building Seven, on the backside, and there were all these huge earthmovers, with seventeen-, eighteen-foot blades, pushing cars out of the way, clearing the street. It was wild. In a matter of about eight or nine hours, equipment was already rolling.

I went around the site and came in from the south, through Liberty Place Park. They were ripping fences down around a city park, just trying to find space. Generators were going up, lights were being set up. By daybreak all four corners of the site were illuminated by some kind of crude lighting.

I walked back to the trailer and there were guys all over the place. Carpenters were building tables and chairs out of rough lumber inside the loading dock. We really didn't discuss anything that first morning, we just signed in.

I was told, "Just go out and do something."

I hooked up with Joe O'Malley, another one of our superintendents. We go out to West Street. I'm looking at Joe, he's looking at me.

I say, "Well, what can we do?"

He says, "I don't know, we have to do something."

Ninety West Street was still burning. There's debris everywhere. The firemen had run hoses all over the place, over the street and up and down stairs. I'm talking miles and miles of hoses. I grabbed some carpenters and said, "Let's pull these hoses over and build a ramp over them." We pulled hoses together and made a raceway for them under the ramps. That way there was a place to put other equipment without putting it on a hose, and a place to safely run more hoses when the firemen needed them. That went on the whole day.

We told the carpenters to start building work sheds. The DDC asked Bovis to build a morgue. Every time I asked somebody to build something, I told them, "Make it movable. Make sure you've got full joists on the bottom so if we have to lift it with a crane and move it the thing doesn't crack in half." That was pretty much it, just shooting off the hip.

At 9 A.M. we had a meeting in the Albany Street trailer. That's when I was given my first specific assignment: to check the perimeter buildings for stability. Ninety West Street was being rehabbed, so there was scaffolding set up around it for the guys who had been working on the façade. But the whole top portion had been bombarded with debris when the South Tower fell. It was hanging loose and needed to come down so it didn't fall down on its own.

Meanwhile firemen are on the north and northeast side of 90 West spraying water on it. We got a crane over there with a jib on it and sent some ironworkers up in a man basket with torches. A man basket is just a big steel box, sort of like a gondola, with steel cables attached to a crane. So it can put guys in places they couldn't otherwise get to, either up in the air, out to the side, or over a barrier. The ironworkers used torches and started cutting the scaffolding loose, just dropping the stuff to the ground—*boom, boom, boom*—then they tied the rest of the scaffolding back to the building with wire.

But there was nothing else we could do. What can you do the first day? Who was in charge? We had a frontend loader ready to march down West Street to clear the street, to move some debris, but a fire truck was in the way. But who's in charge of the fire department, you know?

The firemen were either putting out fires or out on that pile jumping around in and out of every void. They were out there looking for survivors. You couldn't stop them, that was their job. Everybody knew the severity of the collapse, but nobody wanted to believe we were not going to find somebody alive out there. We were thinking, "We've got to go fast, we've got to find what we can find."

The civilians on-site generally fell into place on one of the many bucket brigades that streamed over the pile. They stood for hours—in suits and athletic clothes, work boots, sneakers, and wing tips—passing 40- and 50-pound buckets of material down the line and empty buckets back up. At the head of the brigade, usually, was a group of firemen determining which portion of the pile to remove first—whether to uncover a beam covered with rubble so they could look beneath it or to expose a small void so they could peer inside with a flashlight and, if the opening was large enough, crawl in. Some of this debris was dumped into trucks, but much of it was simply dumped on the ground at the end of the line, wherever space could be found.

When Franciscan Friar Father Brian Jordan learned on September 11 that his mentor and close friend, FDNY chaplain Father Mychal Judge, had died during the Tower collapse, Jordan went to Ground Zero and stayed for most of the next nine months.

FATHER BRIAN JORDAN

I had two choices after I learned that Mychal Judge had died; either sit on my ass and cry, or do what Mychal would have wanted me to do—go down there and see if I could do any good. So that's what I did. I had my holy water in one hand and a pair of brass knuckles in the other—I used to work in the South Bronx and I wasn't sure if I was going to encounter any bad guys along the way. I figured I could bless 'em with one hand and whack 'em with the other if I had to.

I worked the bucket brigade. They couldn't put real heavy equipment on the pile yet because there was still hope that someone might be trapped down below. After two hours my arms were ready to fall off. I said, "I'm not a construction worker, I'm a priest. I bless people with my hands. I'm not used to this. You guys get over here."

But on the pile I saw the most beautiful sight, this New York "can-do" attitude. The bucket brigades were black and white, Latino and Asian, rich and poor, gay and straight, citizens, immigrants, green card holders, whatever—all volunteers coming together, moving those buckets, like an unfinished symphony, wonderful men and women working side by side.

There was so much confusion down there. At first I was just blessing bodies and body parts and talking to firemen and the other workers. I became a lightning rod, a sounding board for their anger at what happened and their frustration over trying to save people and get something accomplished in all the confusion. They'd see me wearing a cross, the brown habit, and the primary question they were asking was "Why did God do this?" In the first ten days, and this is no exaggeration, I was asked that question 500 times.

I told each one that God had nothing to do with this. This was the power of evil, not the power of God.

On a normal construction job, even a demolition project, engineers and architects create drawings and detailed specifications well in advance of the arrival of the workers. Project managers, supervisors, and foremen try to anticipate any contingency. They spend weeks and months working out schedules, equipment, and personnel needs. Everything is planned up front so as to facilitate the safest, most efficient, and cost-effective conditions possible. When all these parameters are in place, the workers arrive, and they are given specific tasks and specific time frames.

They are told, "Don't think, just do."

Ground Zero would be different. In many ways the cleanup would proceed backward and upside down, as people jumped in and began to work wherever, focusing on immediate needs—move this, clear this area, find this machine, solve this small problem and hope doing so will reveal another small achievable goal.

Those on the pile quickly knew more about site conditions than anyone else—it was easy to see from afar where fires still burned; it took another level of understanding altogether to know where you could walk without having your shoes melt or catch on fire. To know which of the beams would hold, which to avoid. To learn where the voids or the crushed stairwells were, where people trying to escape might still be trapped. You had to be on the pile to know which corners might be sheltering survivors and which cradled the dead. The priorities were dynamic and changed by the minute.

Control was degraded not just by the conditions on the site, but by the lack of any coordinated organization or communication between the volunteers, first responders, and the growing number of relief agencies, and state and federal agencies. Cell phones were almost useless. Communication had to take place face-to-face. FDNY had roughly divided the site into sectors, placing their personnel in each sector under the direction of a different fire chief. The FBI declared the site a crime scene and was positioning agents to collect evidence. FEMA, too, was now on the ground, as were the Red Cross and the Salvation Army.

There is no other way to describe it: chaos reigned.

CHARLIE VITCHERS

At the beginning anybody who had any equipment just went where they could and helped out wherever they could. There was just so much confusion and chaos. Who was in charge? Nobody was in charge. Who are you? I don't know who you are. You don't know who I am. I'm doing something, you're doing something. That was the situation. That had to be curtailed.

Early on, people could get in any way they wanted. There were volunteers in white shirts, dress shoes, and suit jackets. Nobody knew who they were, they were just pulling stuff, moving stuff, and working the bucket brigades. The bucket brigade gave these people, most of whom had limited experience in a disaster, the chance to feel like they were doing something. These people wanted to help, and you needed them down there to do what they were doing. You couldn't just sit back and look at the site and not do anything. So we all did something, even if it was wrong.

After the Port Authoriy Police Department (PAPD), NYPD, National Guard, and whoever else was down there finally established a security perimeter around the site, a lot of civilians told me, "I'm not leaving because if I do I know I'm not going to get back in."

I'd say, "You're right. I can't help you out."

It was just as crazy with the union workers. There were too many guys down there, thousands, and somebody was going to get hurt. Some guys said, "Screw you, I'm not going back, I'm staying here until the job is done." We would try to deal with that, maybe give the guy another day. The guy's trying to do the right thing. You didn't want to drag him out of there.

•   •   •

On September 12, amid the chaos, a select group of individuals met at Intermediate School 89, just three blocks north of the site, to take the first steps beyond the present carnage toward a plan. It was an unlikely group, one that in different times likely would have found themselves on opposite sides of the table: construction workers, city agencies, members of the Port Authority, law enforcement personnel, fire department personnel, engineers, and demo experts.

JIM ABADIE, BOVIS

I was in the Bovis trailer all night with my people from our site at the Ritz-Carlton in Battery Park. On the morning of September 12, we got word that we were going to have our first meeting. At 7 A.M., we met with the Department of Design and Construction (DDC), the Office of Emergency Management (OEM), the police department, every emergency company that was down there, and every official company that was down there. We started our control meetings and started going over everything, trying to assess what was going on.

We started trying to figure out what the hell to do, what were the dangers. We knew there were Freon tanks in the pile that could explode and displace oxygen and kill people. Different structures could collapse. The fire department needed cranes to move steel.

There were natural barriers on the site and initially the major contractors moved onto the site where they could. I called up my office and we started drawing up a logistics plan. We decided to cut it up into quads to coordinate the effort.

•   •   •

The "quad" system provided a rudimentary organizational framework. The four major companies selected by the DDC to clean up the site—the construction management firms AMEC, Turner, and Bovis, along with the construction company Tully—roughly divided the site according to where each was able to gain access, and each was given responsibilities for clean-up activities in that quadrant. Tully approached from the east along Church Street, including buildings Five and Four, up to the eastern edge of what had once been the South Tower. Bovis, due to their existing contract at the Ritz-Carlton at the foot of Battery Park City, came in from the southwest and took control of the southern half of the Trade Center site itself, including the South Tower, the Vista Hotel, 90 West Street, and One World Financial. AMEC assumed authority over the northern half of the Trade Center site, the North Tower, Building Six, and World Financial Two and Three; while Turner attacked those areas north of Vesey Street, including Building Seven, Building Six, and the Federal Building.

It was not perfect, but it provided the first measure of control.

CHARLIE VITCHERS

Breaking up the site into quadrants was a great idea, but the DDC should have explained how those quadrants were going to operate, not just say, "Okay, you have this, you have this, you got this, and you got this, and then let's go out and do what we can, guys." To me it was common sense—you couldn't run this site like three or four separate jobs. It wasn't four individual construction sites. It wasn't four individual recovery sites. It was one site.

But something like this had never happened before, and that kind of communication and organization was not taking place. Everybody was looking at that pile wondering if there were people alive or dead. Nobody was really thinking of how to organize what we had down there. It just happened.

As darkness fell on the evening of September 12, only eighteen survivors had been pulled from the ruins. Genelle Guzman-McMillan, a Port Authority employee found in the ruins of the North Tower that afternoon, would be the last.

On the site, thousands toiled on. All had heard stories where survivors of earthquakes or tsunamis or floods were found two, three, even four weeks after the event. In any event, many had already committed themselves to the job; they were not going to leave until it was finished, even if they found no one alive. Finding the dead was no less important.

From the minute the construction workers set foot on the pile, it was all about recovery.

BOBBY GRAY

That second night, I was at the edge of the pile with Sam Melisi of FDNY. I grabbed this operator named Dave who was in Local 15 and asked him to run the Bobcat, a little frontend loader that can hold about a yard of material. He went into the edge of a pile of debris, got a bucket, and backed it up. I don't know where we were thinking we were gonna put the material, but then Sammy said, "Okay, stop him. Just shake it out a little bit. I'm going to go through it."

I'm like, "Huh?"

I'm looking at the pile and then looking at this little bucket of material Sam's sifting through by hand, running it through his fingers. Then I had this realization that we would have to do this with the entire pile, all of it, every single bucket.

I thought, "Oh my God, there's 50,000 people here." We weren't listening to the news or reading the paper. We didn't know how many people were lost there yet. But I already knew we were not going to find many whole people. We were going to find parts, maybe millions of parts, and if there were 50,000 people in the pile, I knew two of them might be in this bucket.

CHARLIE VITCHERS

I was on the loading dock at One World Financial Center at about 8 P.M. and a fireman came in and he asked me if I had a Sawzall blade—that's a small, straight blade for a power utility saw used a lot on demolition. You can use it to cut through Sheetrock, studs, things like that.

I told him, "I've got a whole case of Sawzall's, brand new in the boxes. I think they're on the pier over there."

He says, "I need something *now*. You got a hacksaw blade?"

"I don't," I said. "But there's a superintendent's shanty right around the corner. It's padlocked; you got bolt cutters?"

And the guy said, real serious, "Yeah, I'll get you bolt cutters."

He comes back two minutes later with a pair of bolt cutters, and *bang*, we break into the shanty. We go into the back and there are a bunch of file cabinets with locks on them. *Snap, snap, snap,* we opened them up and eventually found hacksaw blades.

I say, "You want the hacksaw too, or do you just want the blade?"

He goes, "Just the blade. Do you have any duct tape?"

"Duct tape we got plenty of," I said.

So we go back into the loading dock and I hand the guy a roll of duct tape and ask, "What else you need?"

He goes, "That's it, that's it," and he takes off.

About an hour and a half later I walk out onto the site in front of the Vista Hotel. Here's this same fireman all by himself and I ask him, "What's going on?"

He said, "I'm just doing what I gotta do, man."

He had wrapped duct tape around the hacksaw blade for a handle and he's sawing at this piece of aluminum skin that had covered the façade of the Trade Center—it's only like an eighth of an inch thick—that had come off the façade steel and laid down flat. The fireman had found a woman's body pinned under this ⅛-inch-thick piece of aluminum. There was a box beam laying over it one way, and other steel laying over it the other way, and this woman was underneath. The only thing stopping him from getting her out was this little bitty, thin piece of fucking aluminum. I didn't realize what he was even doing at first. Then I finally saw what I saw, and it blew me away. He cut through the aluminum, took off a five-foot section, and there she was, dead. It was so wild. He turned around and I said to him, "WOW, you need some help?"

He goes, "No, I just want to make sure that we get her out without destroying anything else that's around here. We're going to take out what we can. I want to see if we can find the rest of her."

This guy was alone. He didn't even have another fireman with him. He was doing this on his own. He had the patience to sit there and saw with his hand rather than screaming for a crane to lift this and lift that and tear stuff up. He found this woman and he went ahead and he spent hours on her before I came and found him.

I don't remember the guy's name, but I wish I could find him now. I'll never forget that. She was dead, but he wanted to make sure that her body didn't suffer any more damage. I just think that was amazing.

She wasn't even in the pile. She was still half-on and half-off of West Street, probably just somebody walking down the road or running for her life. Who knows? You look at the pile and then you turn and look at the Winter Garden and you think of the people who were running into that building. And here I was on West Street, just looking down the highway. The enormity of this whole thing hit me. Forget about what's in the pile for a second . . . just look at what we have on the highway. And that's not even a drop in the bucket compared to what we have in the pile.

God help us with what we're going to find in the pile.

CHAPTER FOUR

ONTO THE PILE

Seventy-two hours after the attacks, the area surrounding the Trade Cen-
ter had been transformed: a construction site had emerged to wrap its arms
around the disaster. Hundreds of vehicles, removed from the perimeter of
the site, sat stacked like cordwood several stories high on nearby side
streets. Thousands of tons of loose debris encircling the site had been
removed and dumped wherever space was available, awaiting removal by
truck. Corridors had been cut through the debris on West Street and
Church Street and both were now passable to construction traffic, as
were portions of Vesey and Liberty Streets. The Fresh Kills Landfill in
Staten Island had been reopened to accept truckloads of debris, and the U.S.
Army Corps of Engineers would soon begin dredging the river so material
could be transferred by barge. Access to the site was increasing by the hour
and heavy equipment was beginning to arrive.

Vital work had been accomplished in the immediate aftermath of the
collapse, but bare hands, bulldozers, bucket brigades, and forklifts had
reached an impasse. Mammoth steel columns, ejected from the Towers dur-
ing the collapse, littered the site. The twisted remnants of the Tower façades
reached some 200 feet into the sky, an eerie gothic silhouette that would
become known as the shrouds. The bulk of the pile was a massed jumble of
crushed concrete, steel cable, shattered glass, and amorphous hulks of
forged metal, spiked deep into the subterranean levels. The answers to the
most basic questions—how to move forward, what equipment would be

needed, where to start, when, who would be coordinating—were as yet ill-defined, obscured by fatigue and buried beneath disorder.

Part of the reason the pile was so resistant to delivering clear answers was the structural design of the Towers themselves. Before construction of the Twin Towers, skyscrapers were built of a robust steel matrix of columns and beams running from bottom to top, like interlocking stacks of steel-framed cubes. Each individual vertical column was placed directly upon the column below and tied to those alongside by horizontal beams. The same basic pattern was repeated on each floor.

The result was an incredibly strong structure, but each floor was pierced every fifteen or twenty feet by a column, which dramatically reduced rentable floor space. The taller the building, the worse the problem became, for the more weight a column had to support, the bigger it had to be. While the technology existed to build even taller buildings, it wasn't economically feasible.

Structural engineers came up with an innovative design for the Twin Towers. The buildings would be supported by massive columns concentrated in the core with additional support provided by exterior columns on the perimeter that also doubled as its decorative façade. The core columns and exterior columns were then connected by steel trusses that supported the reinforced concrete floor decks. The result was that much of the interior floor space was column-free.

But the 9/11 attacks revealed a serious problem with the design: as heat from the fires weakened the steel floor trusses on the upper floors, they slumped. This additional stress caused the connections between the columns and the trusses to fail, dropping the floor onto the floor directly below. The trusses and connections on that floor, also stressed and weakened by heat, couldn't support the additional weight. No one had foreseen the possibility of one floor "pancaking" directly on top of another. The failure set up a massive chain reaction, as floor after floor broke loose from both the core columns and the exterior columns.

The amount of steel and concrete that came crashing down in the col-

lapse is almost incomprehensible. Most outsiders, along with those already working on the site, initially believed that cranes would remove the bulk of the material. Starting on the first night, a number of small 40- to 80-ton rubber-tired cranes worked the perimeter of the pile, clearing roads and picking loose steel from as far into the pile as they could reach. Once the roads were clear, it seemed reasonable to move in massive cranes—those weighing up to one million pounds—to more or less surround the site, reach in and over, and slowly bring the pile down to grade. Once they were at grade, the cranes would move onto the pile itself.

Load by load, incredible amounts of steel would be hoisted away from the pile and onto waiting trucks, which would then off-load the material onto barges anchored on the Hudson River. The barges—capable of carrying 150,000 tons at a time—would take the debris to the Fresh Kills Landfill. There, it would be meticulously searched to ensure no remains were lost. Logical, rational, coordinated.

But it would not be that simple. Nothing at Ground Zero would ever be simple.

BOBBY GRAY

My first reaction to the pile was that we had to get cranes because we were going to have massive amounts of steel coming out of that hole.

Early on, we had some big cranes there. One with a 1,000-ton maximum capacity, one with an 800-ton capacity, and one with 500 tons, as well as a bunch of 250-ton capacity cranes. Some of them were so big they came to the site on eighteen or twenty trailers, in pieces, and we had to set them up.

Lifting capacity depends on the configuration of the crane, the length of your boom, and the boom angle. In conventional crane mode, which is what you'd see at a normal job site, the boom on the crane sticks up in the air at a 70 degree angle. When it's configured like that you can lift, or what we call pick, until the crane itself actually starts to lift up in the back, reaching its tipping capacity. As soon as that happens, you have to be a lot more careful. If what you are picking is too heavy it can pull the crane over, or if whatever you've hooked into suddenly breaks loose and comes out fast, it can throw you back, like when one side lets go in a game of tug-of-war.

At the Trade Center, most operators just kept pulling and pulling and pulling on a piece of steel until it came up or the crane was right up on its toes, tilted up on its tracks. You don't see that done on a regular job.

But what operators really have to be careful of is their reach—how far out the crane is reaching. The farther they're reaching, the lower the angle, which lowers capacity.

We had to use chokers, steel cable, to wrap around whatever we were trying to move. They all have capacities themselves, depending on the diameter of the cable, how many are used, whether they are basketed like a sling, or whether they're actually choked, which is when you put the steel eye of the choker through another eye of the choker. If you exceed the capacity of the choker and the choker parts, the crane can go over backwards, too. So we also had to know what kinds of chokers to use, what their capacity was, what they were good for. We would take the cranes to 100 percent capacity sometimes trying to make a pick and it still wouldn't move. If you hooked into a column and you couldn't budge it, the ironworkers would just cut out as much of the column as they could, cut the piece and make it smaller. Again, it was like a game of pick-up sticks. "Let's see what we have to move to get to here. This piece of steel is holding me up from getting that piece of steel." That's pretty much how it went. Even the 800-ton and 1,000-ton cranes tried to make some pulls that just wouldn't move.

Some of those box columns were more than 30 feet tall and weighed 60 tons. The plates were probably two, two and a half inches thick. Some were four feet by two feet, some were more square in shape, like two by two, or four by four. A lot of columns were wider than they were deep. It would take the ironworkers a good hour just to cut through a column.

Ironworkers have always worked with the cranes. That's one of their specialties, that's what they know the best, rigging up steel so we can move it. Most of us had worked with the ironworkers and were very comfortable with them, especially me.

The ironworkers were tremendously important to the entire operation at Ground Zero. An essential group at the initial construction of the Towers, many of these same men arrived on the pile within hours of the attack on September 11, 2001. Like so many of the trades, the ironworkers have a long history in New York. And like so many New Yorkers, their story begins elsewhere.

Along the rocky coast of the Canadian province of Newfoundland, small fishing villages known as outports cling to the shore between the highlands and the sea. Most of these isolated towns, perhaps thirty or forty spare houses, are populated by a few hundred hardy, close-knit residents. In any one outport there are rarely more than a half-dozen Irish surnames in the church graveyard—Murphys and Whelans, Murrays and Kellys. Nearly everyone is somehow related.

For generations, there has been little work in Newfoundland apart from that provided by the sea. In the spring, as soon as the sea ice breaks free, men take to the water in small boats known as dories, picking their way through the ever-present fog of the frigid North Atlantic to fish for cod, casting nets over the swells, hauling their catch in by hand, then drying and salting it in the sun on rare "fine" days.

Deep into the twentieth century, many Newfoundlanders still lived a life grounded in another age, without electricity, telephones, or plumbing. Automobiles were rare and roads were made of gravel. Whatever day the priest arrived by boat became Sunday. Houses were lit with oil lamps, and during the long, dark winters the only bit of warmth to be had was from the wood stove in the kitchen—and a bottle of potent rum known as Newfie Screech.

The dust, grit, and impersonal, mechanized anarchy of a New York construction site are worlds away from life in an outport town. But for generations, some Newfoundlanders, in search of a better life, have made that pilgrimage, traveling to New York City to work in the trades. Iron-work has long been their preferred choice. Frankly, compared to the dangers of sailing alone in the North Atlantic, standing hundreds of feet above the ground on a steel beam hardly seems more dangerous—and the pay is far better.

The first of these men commuted to New York as seasonal workers, returning to Newfoundland in the dead of winter when work was slow. Dubbed fish by others in the trade, some eventually decided to move their families permanently to New York, many settling in the Bay Ridge neighborhood of Brooklyn. Over time, sons followed fathers into the trade. Although that tradition, like the cod fishery itself, has begun to fade, there are still some fish in Local 40, the ironworkers' union in New York City.

Willie Quinlan's father, of Conception Bay, Newfoundland, was a fish who traveled to New York for seasonal work before permanently moving his family to Brooklyn. And like his father, Willie Quinlan is an ironworker in Local 40.

WILLIE QUINLAN, IRONWORKER

My father started coming here in about 1959 or 1960. He took our whole family here in 1962, when I was fifteen.

It was a big, big change for me, coming from Newfoundland to Brooklyn. Everything was different. At times it was pretty hard. He didn't want me or my three brothers to go into construction, but we did it anyway. I didn't want to go to college so I went to ironwork instead. Paddy works in Newfoundland for the government now. Tommy is retired from ironwork, and my brother Ray is in the carpenter's union.

I started as an apprentice. Back then the job was to keep the journeymen busy—getting them any necessary tools or supplies, getting their coffee for them, and water. I had to get all the tools out in the morning and bring all the tools in at the end of the evening.

I'd been around ironwork all my life and it came to me pretty naturally. You just watch and you look and you say, "I can do that," and then you just start doing it. As an apprentice, you climb on everything. One of my first jobs in New York was in Madison Square Garden. I was in the business only two or three years before I went to work on the Trade Center. I was a journeyman there, on the North Tower, the first one that went up.

It was a great job, the biggest job in the world at the time. I was honored to have an opportunity like that, and I met so many great ironworkers who I had heard about through my family. The old-timers were really an important part of the learning day. They showed you how to work. Everybody had different ideas and ways to do things and it gave me an opportunity to look and weigh everything out. You don't learn in school what you learn in the field.

The Trade Center Towers were one of a kind, each was a square box. The heaviest iron was on the perimeter of the building and in the core, where it carried the elevators. From the core of the building to the perimeter were 40 by 20 panels that formed the floor deck and connected the core and perimeter together. The panels were made out of decking and bar joists and they sat on very limber lugs on the perimeter of the building, which held everything together—⅝-inch bolts. The old-timers thought the deck was flimsy compared to the heavy iron in the core and the outside, but you needed that to carry the structure.

It wasn't really a sturdy structure as far as we were concerned. You could see it wasn't such a great design. If you're going to pile 110 floors on top of each other you've got to have something to hold it.

I worked there for seven years from start to finish, so it was just a natural instinct that you had to go down there, because you knew when those buildings came down that there had to be steel all over the place.

For both men and machines, working on the pile or near it was hazardous. As yet there was no way of knowing if surrounding streets could support the biggest cranes and whether they could be staged close enough to be used efficiently. No one knew, for certain, what lay beneath the surface debris on the pile, whether the wreckage created a stable surface or covered massive voids. Even walking on the debris was dangerous. Somehow, they needed to gain a three-dimensional perspective of the entire area.

CHARLIE VITCHERS

You'd walk thirty feet into the pile and the debris pile would shake up and down on you, like walking on a wooden bridge or a suspension bridge. You didn't know if you had a void below, so you had to be very careful. You knew it wasn't safe for a 100,000-pound machine, or anything heavier.

As soon as we started to bring in the cranes, we needed the engineers. Any time that you bring a crane into New York, even if you want to roll it down 6th Avenue, you have to get the engineering to make sure that you're on ground that can support the weight of that load. The engineers became very concerned when all of a sudden we were erecting cranes and preparing to move them into the site.

PETER RINALDI, PORT AUTHORITY, ENGINEER

We did a lot of the mapping belowground. What we were looking for was the actual condition of the area that was belowground, subgrade. Remember, there were six levels belowground on the site. Were they fully collapsed? We had teams of engineers trying to go down belowground, map out and inspect what it looked like, and try to ascertain what was solid and intact and where there was structure that was not collapsed. What we tried to do is get that information on each of the basement levels and then draw up maps that we updated daily. We posted maps of each level on the wall in IS 89. Green areas were intact. Red were fully collapsed. Pink were kind of in between.

We knew what was going to happen above grade and wanted to

make it safe for the recovery and rescue teams. That's how we used that information.

Periodically we would get called out from someone like Sam Melisi from the fire department. He'd say, "You know, we're thinking about going in here to search." But the operators would tell him, "I'm not so sure we can go in there." So an engineer would go out and look and say either, "No you can't be in there" or "This is okay. Here it's solid."

RICHARD GARLOCK, ENGINEER

I am a structural engineer at Leslie E. Robertson Associates (LERA). I started work the summer after the 1993 WTC bombing. I learned all about the Trade Center, both Towers, the sub-grade levels, and the slurry wall—the foundation that contains the site. Our office also did regular structural integrity inspections of the slurry wall, the sub-grade structures, the whole complex. Over the years, I would periodically go back to do that. I was building this encyclopedia in my mind about the Trade Center. Our firm had an unbelievable amount of firsthand knowledge and the original drawings and documents about the area.

In 1993, within hours of the bombing, the police came to our office and said, "We need you." We were expecting that kind of response after 9/11, but there was organizational disarray from day one. The people that knew we had valuable information were in total disarray. We tried to call everybody we could—the police department, the fire department, the FBI, ATF, FEMA, Port Authority. We told them, "Here we are, we have useful information," but nobody was responding.

I didn't arrive at Ground Zero until almost a week after the attacks when the Structural Engineers of New York (SEANY), a professional group, was organizing volunteers. Then, a few days later, LERA had a formal presence and I stayed there all the way through, until the end.

When we first went out underground in four-man engineering teams, we were escorted by the NYPD's Emergency Services Unit. Then FDNY took over. To the best of our abilities, we got to everywhere we could get to. But already, virtually all those areas had already been searched for survivors.

We were trying to determine where there was intact structure belowground, because as contractors moved inside the foundation wall, there were areas of compacted debris and areas that were intact. From a bird's-eye view aboveground, it all looked the same, but some areas had solid footing and some areas did not. I was able to tell guys like Charlie, "Hey, better keep equipment away from here, it's not safe."

And therein lay the problem. There simply was not enough intact structure belowground to support large machinery on the pile itself. Although cranes continued to operate from the perimeter, none could be set up within the foundation walls. Some areas of the pile were simply beyond their reach. And even in the areas they could get to, cranes—while adept at picking steel—were much less efficient at removing loose rubble.

What then? The solution came from the men and women working on the pile. Even as mappers were still surveying underground levels, operators were already using a machine known as a grappler on the pile.

A grappler is a powerful excavator with an incredibly dexterous hydraulic arm. The end of the arm is fitted not with a bucket, but a hydraulically operated, articulating set of tines—a claw—that grasps rather than scoops. Not only do grapplers roll over virtually any terrain on large steel caterpillar tracks, which distribute their weight over a wide area, they can grasp loose material as well as steel columns without the rigging required by a larger crane. They are quick, adaptable, and powerful, and they were absolutely essential at Ground Zero. Skilled operators worked the hydraulic arm like an extension of their own body.

Watching the grapplers in action, Bobby Gray, Charlie Vitchers, and the FDNY quickly realized that the machines' ability to move onto the pile and grasp material delicately, like a hand, made it uniquely suited for the job. Very quickly, the grappler emerged as the mechanical workhorse of the cleanup.

BOBBY GRAY

One day the realization came that cranes were just not going to be as useful as the grapplers. That was huge. I watched a grappler and he could actually walk the machine closer and closer and even get up on the pile.

I knew the machines existed, but they're used mostly in junkyards and on demolition jobs and I hadn't done any demolition jobs. Watching the grapplers was a revelation. I was blown away by what the operators could do with them.

Depending on the size of the machine and how far out the operator was reaching with the boom, a grappler could either grab two or three yards of loose material or move a 10-ton or even a 20-ton column without any problem. If they couldn't lift it, they'd roll it or drag it. At one point up on Liberty Street I kept hearing this *BOOM! BOOM! BOOM!* And here comes a grappler with a box column. He couldn't pick it up, but he could roll it over on the side, *BOOM!*, then pick it up and roll it again, *BOOM!*

I don't care if you've worked in construction for one hundred years, you've never seen anything like this. I saw some of these guys do things that were just incredible. I was just so proud. They floored me with how precise they were and even how dainty they could be when they needed to. One night, when some steel shifted, a fireman got pinned underneath and broke his leg pretty bad. They brought a grappler operator over. Like a surgeon, he was able to come in with his grappler and remove this huge piece of steel off this fireman's leg without doing any more damage. How could he do that without crushing him? It was miraculous.

I saw this one guy just pick apart the Vista Hotel, one column at a time. He was teeter-tottering, up on the toes of the machine and rocking the whole building. I was thinking, "If it snaps towards that grappler, he's gone. There's no way he can get away—there's just too much steel." But he was able to rock it back and forth and when it looked like it was ready to go, he just pushed it all away from him. I just couldn't fathom how you could even think about doing something like that.

JIM ABADIE, BOVIS

In the beginning it was the top down saying, "You've got to do it this way." But after we got feedback from the trades, we said, "No, we've got to do it this way." I realized pretty quickly it wasn't just a steel removal job, but a demo job. We wouldn't just be picking steel with cranes, but removing material by other means. It just wasn't obvious in the beginning.

CHARLIE VITCHERS

Before the Towers came down the inferno that was going on in the upper levels completely burned anything that was on the upper levels both where the planes crashed and probably the two floors below. But jet fuel had poured down the elevator shafts and into the basement. My guess is that just about that whole building, more than you could see on TV, was on fire, internally, before it actually collapsed. The cameras focused mainly on where the planes entered the Towers and on the fireball, but there was a lot more on fire before those buildings came down. When the Towers collapsed down into the lower levels, everything that was combustible down there burned, like the automobiles in the underground garages, the ruptured gas tanks.

The fires were very intense on the pile, the heat was very intense. In some places you couldn't even get onto it. In some areas where you could walk, you'd travel another five feet and then you could just feel the heat coming up and you would have to just back off. You'd say to yourself, "I can't see a fire, but I can feel the heat, so something's wrong here," and you'd back off.

That was one of the concerns we had about putting equipment on the pile, because the operators were sitting eight or ten feet up above the debris pile in their cabs and couldn't feel the heat. But they're carrying a hundred gallons of diesel fuel, hydraulic hoses, and other flammables, and there was nothing to stop the heat from wrecking the machine. If they got stuck in a place where the heat was so intense that it set his machine on fire, that operator wasn't going to make it out.

We were so lucky. We didn't lose anyone. We lost a lot of equipment, mostly due to collapses, but didn't have any piece of equipment catch on fire or anything like that. But hoses melted, and there was a lot of damage to tires—some of them melted just from being too close. I mean, the bottom of your shoes would melt on some of the steel. Some of that was so hot you could feel the hair on the back of your neck start to burn when you walked by. There were cherry-red pieces of steel sticking out of the ground. It was almost like being in a steel-manufacturing plant. You just couldn't physically go near that stuff.

Every time a grappler grabbed a piece of steel and shook it out, it would just fan the fire, like a fan in the fireplace. All of a sudden there'd be smoke billowing out.

The Army Corp of Engineers eventually supplied us with infrared aerial shots of where the heat was. It was like looking at the blob. The fire was *moving* under the pile. One day it would be hot here, it would be 1,400 degrees, and the next day it would be 2,000 degrees, and then five days later it wouldn't register over 600 degrees.

What they said to me was that concrete contains air pockets of oxygen and silica, and the silica will burn. The fire kept feeding on itself. It was like throwing a rock in the fire. It explodes. At the end they determined that most of the concrete just kept popping and popping and popping to the point where it was pulverized into dust.

The work was terrible on the machines. They ripped treads out, blew tires, broke lights—forget about it. If an operator turned and smacked a piece of steel, it could ruin the whole deck platform. They'd roll over a steel beam and the leg would kick down and a beam would come up into the oil pan of the machine or rip some hydraulic hoses off. Now all of a sudden the arm drops and there's no hydraulic control of the machine. That stuff just doesn't happen on a normal job.

We had a guy, his name was Jimmy Chisano, with a big 1200 grappler, the biggest grappler on-site, who grabbed a piece of steel and squeezed it, went to move it, and the whole grappler arm just shattered in half and broke off. That shit doesn't happen in the real world, but when you stress a machine like that constantly twenty-four hours a day, something's going to give.

BOBBY GRAY

The majority of the grapplers did the same thing from day one until the last grappler was there. Their principal job was to get up on the pile, remove material, and assist with recoveries. They probably assisted in 90 percent of the recoveries, maybe even 99 percent of the recoveries, because most of the remains were found in the pile.

Depending on the way the wind was blowing, the grapplers would sometimes just disappear. The smoke was that bad. The fire department was constantly just spraying water on the pile, hoping that it would seep through to where the main heat was. I remember pulling columns up that were cherry red. Especially at night, that was incredible to see. A 30-foot column carried high above the ground would be cherry red. It wasn't in a molten stage, but it was certainly too hot to put on a truck because the truck beds are all wood. We'd have to leave it on the side to cool. Sometimes the fire trucks would come by and hose them down.

From the start, we worked very closely with the fire department. A lot of times we did things we probably shouldn't have, but we wanted to. If a fireman asked for help, 99 percent of the time the operators would back off from what he was supposed to be doing and try to help the guy with a recovery. If they found a void, for example, we'd go over there and dig around a little bit and open it up.

In the beginning, we just tried to get them as close as possible to the debris, clear enough space to get a truck in, then load the trucks directly with the grappler. As we got farther in, the grapplers daisy-chained debris off the pile, literally passing it from machine to machine. If you had four grapplers, number one was reaching into the pile, swinging 180 degrees to grappler two, who was taking the material another 180 degrees to grappler three, then on to grappler four. As they swung around, they'd open the jaws to spread out what was in them. If there was room, it would be searched, or else the next machine would grab what the first machine had and spread it out again. It gave the firemen a real good look at what was coming out of an area. Eventually we were able to set up something like a transfer station. Debris would get daisy-chained to a certain area, then searched for remains and loaded into the trucks.

Most of the firemen had never worked in such close proximity to heavy equipment. If you're not familiar with being around the equipment, it's not a place to be. That was a huge concern, because it was dangerous. A lot of close relationships developed between certain gangs of firemen and my operators. The fire department tried to keep the same gang of spotters with the same crane. Then when their men rotated out they would actually have a class for the new guys coming into the site. Usually, recovery workers lined up to the right of the boom, to stay in the vision of the operator. We got that down pretty quick.

The bodies of firemen were easier to spot because a lot of times they had their bunker gear on or their helmet nearby. Their bunker gear sometimes held their remains together. All the other remains were actually hard to see. As much as I tried not to see it, you couldn't help seeing it.

Some of the grappler operators were almost like cadaver dogs. They would tell the firemen, "I smell something. I can smell something, it's over here." That was a sad thing for them to experience, but at the same time it was a good thing.

Whenever an operator found a body, we'd get ahold of someone from FDNY. All nearby work would stop and a crew of firemen would come down with little garden tools and just try and excavate by hand to see what exactly was there or, unfortunately, how much was there.

While the command structure of the fire department was still reeling from the loss of life that decimated the department, several members of the FDNY quickly assumed a key role on the pile, facilitating communication between those searching for bodies on the pile and the construction workers. As yet, although both groups were working at the same place at the same time, there was no formal mechanism for either group to know or understand what the other group was doing or why. Firemen focused on recovery didn't understand why a crane operator was picking steel in one place when the firemen wanted to search in another. Neither did all the construction workers yet understand the search strategies of the firemen. It would take weeks, even months before the two groups fully understood what the other was doing.

Three firefighters who arrived on-site shortly after the Towers collapsed—Michael Banker, Steve Rasweiler, and Sam Melisi—took it upon themselves to act as liaisons and points of contact between the two groups. During the next nine months they never rotated off-site but remained at the Trade Center full-time, gaining vast knowledge of all facets of the cleanup and recovery operation and providing critical continuity. Melisi in particular—a former crane operator who was a member of an FDNY task force that had gone to Oklahoma City during the recovery operation at the Murrah Building—was able to communicate with both his FDNY commanders and the construction workers, facilitating the efficient flow of information between both groups.

The learning curve on the pile was steep, and anyone who arrived even a week or ten days after the attacks was often hopelessly behind and struggled to catch up. Those who were there from the start—Charlie Vitchers, Bobby Gray, Jim Abadie, Mike Banker, Sam Melisi, Steve Rasweiler—became indispensable.

CHARLIE VITCHERS

I could always find Stevie, Sam, and Mike or Stevie or Mike or Sam. One of them was always there, twenty-four hours a day. Between the three of those guys, FDNY always had the job site covered.

Sammy and I became very, very close on that job site. I think that's because the two of us felt that we were both there more for our own need to be there to help than to work for the people we were working for. Sammy wanted to remove everybody that had died down there with dignity and respect, and I felt the same way, so it was very easy for Sam and I to get along and approach things together, work things out together.

As far as I was concerned Sammy was the number one guy with the fire department down there, but he was just a firefighter, he wasn't a commander. He wasn't even assigned to be down there doing what he was doing. Before 9/11 he worked on a fire boat in the marine division. But whenever I had a problem down there and I needed fire brass to make a decision, Sammy got the brass to come and see me. I got that respect from Sammy, Sammy got it back from me so that we were always, always on the same page. Sammy always wanted to be involved with excursions, taking people down below grade, because he was interested to see where the changes were taking place down below the bottom of the pile and to look for survivors. I'd go down there with him and we'd shut off all the equipment and listen.

RICHARD GARLOCK, ENGINEER

Sam was someone I could go to. He was there all the time. Before I met him, I would have to go all around the site to the fire department command huts and try to talk with the chiefs. As engineers, we knew we could help them know where they were in the debris pile, give them drawings and explain that to them. But as soon as I'd get some rapport with a chief, he would be rotated out. That's why Sam was important. He was a constant presence. Sam trusted me and would vouch for me. Now the chief wouldn't have to evaluate me and see if I was for real. Sam reduced my frustration level considerably.

Charlie started to fill that role on the contractor's end. He was savvy enough to understand that the engineers had a lot of information to offer, and that working together was a whole lot better than just thinking about how many tons of material are getting out each day. He wanted to know how things could be done best and how we could protect people and still get things done. He recognized the value of people. There were some other supervisors I would go to and not have any confidence that what I said would be acted upon, and I didn't want to waste my time with people who wouldn't act. I knew Charlie understood the value of what the engineers and everybody else had to say.

The quad system slowly began to exert some rudimentary control over the site. By the end of the first week to ten days, most volunteers had been sent home and most workers were assigned to some authority, divvied up between contractors. Clearly, everyone would have to be paid, for neither the workers nor the contractors could work for free forever. The possibility of survivors made any bid process untenable—no one wanted to face the question that anyone went undiscovered and died because of a time-consuming bureaucratic requirement.

With the Federal Emergency Management Agency (FEMA) supplying the funds, FEMA, the DDC, and the construction industry reached a quick agreement to turn what had been a volunteer effort into a paying job with all the attendant controls that required. The cleanup was treated as a "time and materials" job, akin to the process that takes place on a normal job whenever a task beyond the scope of an existing contract is encountered. Rather than bid out the new chore and cause work to grind to a halt, contractors are often allowed to add the additional cost of labor and materials to the existing contract. This solution allowed work to continue without cessation.

With some small exceptions, the workers would be paid standard union wages, while the major contractors would simply submit bills for payroll, equipment, and materials. Eventually, a 1.5 percent profit would be added to those costs. But for the firms involved, this would not be a lucrative job. Profit margins were much higher on normal projects far less complicated and problematic, and this was a job that as yet had no schedule and was impacting those jobs already under way elsewhere.

CHARLIE VITCHERS

From the first day, none of the guys ever even thought they were going to get paid. Guys just came down and hopped on equipment, grabbed hoses, hooked up lights, moved things, built things. They were on a mission. When they found out they were going to get paid, they were happy because they wanted to be there, and now it was legal for them to be there. Everybody knew you couldn't keep working as volunteers.

Under usual union rules, in between each eight-hour shift there's a twenty-minute knock-down period for the re-oiling of machines and maintenance. But with three shifts we wouldn't have had equipment working twenty-four hours a day. So the trades worked twelve-hour shifts. The normal day is seven hours of straight time, and anything after that is overtime. But the unions said, "We'll give that up." A deal was worked out so they'd get eight hours of straight time and four hours of overtime on each shift.

With a twelve-hour shift, everybody got something they wanted. Each piece of equipment worked eleven hours each shift. That meant we had an hour to oil it, grease it, change the tires, do whatever we had to do. That kept equipment working.

Another reason we went to two shifts instead of three is because if you had three seven-hour shifts, you'd only have twenty-one hours of work each day, and you would need three times the number of people. Triple shifts would have wiped out work on half of the other buildings under construction in New York, and the economy needed that work to go on.

Bovis's negotiations with the unions were done through Jim Abadie on our behalf. I believe that set the precedent.

As the days and nights stretched into a long chain of rolling twelve-hour shifts, the men and women who labored on the pile itself—construction workers and firemen, policemen and engineers—began to ease into a tentative collaboration with one another. The workers on the pile were making partnerships that would continue to grow over the next nine months. Never, however, would any of them be allowed to lose sight of what the job was. The pile wouldn't let them.

CHARLIE VITCHERS

At one point in time we realized we were all spotters until you see something, then you're a recovery worker. Everybody was always looking, you know, or listening. The first few weeks you were looking and listening. A lot of times the construction workers found the bodies first. Even if the fire department had already been in an area, the ironworkers were out there burning steel and they'd find something.

We could spend hours on just one extraction. First, we'd move everything we could see immediately, all the debris. We might bring the grappler in and take a three-pack out, which is what we called three beams tied together with a spandrel or a joist, then get this box beam out of the way. Then the rescue workers went to work.

The construction workers and the rescue workers were the only people down there looking for remains. Ninety percent of the guys who went to these administrative meetings sat from afar. They didn't know what that was like for us.

Looking for recoveries wasn't my job either, right? But I was down there and I made it my job. I was looking all the time. Everybody was looking all the time.

What scared me down there in the initial days was nobody knew how many people had died down there. We weren't watching TV or reading the newspaper, and nobody was telling us how many people were there. The initial rumors were that more than 50,000 people might be in that pile. That made me automatically say, "Hey, this is going to take whatever it takes." We couldn't just rip and tear into this pile. We just couldn't. Later on, when I found out that the count might only be 3,000 to 7,000 people, did it make me feel any better? No. Because I knew, looking at this pile, that even if only 200 people were spread around this pile, we were going to have to find everything, everybody that we could. We were going to have to sift through this pile, literally on our hands and knees.

I knew there was light ahead, though. Did I have a time frame for it? Not at all. But I knew it could be done. I knew that we could organize it to remove all of the debris and recover the bodies. Everybody that was in that site that we could find, we were going to find them. As far as a time frame, I didn't put time frames on anything until maybe late November. But as far as the overall site? I had no idea how long it was going to take.

I wanted to get up on the pile and I wanted to find whoever I could. During my initial days down there I was hoping to find somebody alive, so anytime I saw any remains of the deceased, I just walked past it, and made a mental note of it or I jotted it down and told myself, "Later on I'm going to report that there are body parts here, body parts there." I just kept moving. When I saw something, I'd have to look at it real close to realize it's even a body part. You'd look at it, and look at it, and then finally realize what you're looking at.

It didn't make me sick. It made me real sad.

CHAPTER FIVE

THE SLURRY WALL

To anyone who looked at Ground Zero from a distance, the most striking feature of the pile remained those portions of the Tower facades that had survived the collapse. Towering 200 feet above the ruins, the charred black skeletons created a sacred silhouette.

The façade of the South Tower was particularly impressive, stretching twenty stories into the air. The entire structure looked like some kind of postapocalyptic cathedral, jagged, twisted, and bent. It loomed over the pile and, to those unfamiliar with construction sites, seemed to present a clear threat to anyone working below.

Yet although some of the upper portions visibly swung back and forth, the shrouds were far more robust than they appeared.

Their real significance was symbolic. They had become icons of the destruction of September 11, and of the tremendous loss of innocent life. Rising from the debris, to many the shrouds were a symbol not of American grief, but of American resolve: Fuck you, you'll never win. We're Americans.

But to a few key site administrators, the shrouds represented something entirely different. They were an affront. Although their continuing presence did not impede the ongoing efforts to recover victims, they were a constant reminder of what remained to be carted off. Only days after the attacks, Mike Burton of the DDC told the mayor's office he hoped to have the site down to grade by the end of the year, a deadline that coincided with the end of Mayor Giuliani's term. Among the bureaucracies and agencies running the site, taking down the Tower façades as quickly as possible was becoming something of an obsession. Their removal would be seen as a visible sign of progress far more compelling than the sight of truck after truck, loaded with loose debris, leaving the site.

And so the first attempt to pull down the South Tower took place on September 25.

CHARLIE VITCHERS

We had surveyors set up sight lines to see if the shrouds were moving and collapse was imminent. We picked out a crucible on the South Tower, around the fifteenth floor, and we told a guy, "You stare at that. You take a reading every twenty minutes. We want a report every hour."

And what did he report? It would move three-eighths of an inch south and then three-eighths of an inch north. The thing wasn't doing anything more than just blowing in the wind. It wasn't about to come down.

So okay, let's come up with a plan of how we're going to demolish it now.

Somewhere in the mix this guy Dave Griffin, a demolition consultant, and his crew came in with all their brilliant ideas. The initial conversation began with the question, "Well, what do we do with that southwest façade of the South Tower? It's in our quadrant. What are we going to do with it, how are we going to take it down?" We'd sit down at this table and we'd go over it. The ironworkers had their ideas and we kicked around a bunch of them and we came up with different plans.

What we should have done was left the damn thing alone and let the ironworkers take it down the way they wanted to.

Griffin originally put explosives on the table. I kid you not. Yes, we could have detonated this wall and taken it down in one shot. But we were not putting explosives in this pile. We weren't going to blow up the remains of humans in this pile for the sake of expediting the demolition. Sorry, it ain't happening.

That the idea was entertained at all was because the DDC wanted the site down as fast as it could go. They had to answer to City Hall, and Michael Burton told Mayor Giuliani he'd have this site down to grade by New Year's Day.

Griffin had the DDC's ear, so there was a tug-of-war. I would sit with his expert, we'd come up with a methodology and a plan to do something, and then Griffin would have what he thought was a better idea. So we'd have to go back to the table.

Working with the ironworkers, we came up with a methodology of cutting it down—a plan we called giving it a haircut. We would lift the ironworkers up there by crane in man baskets and just cut it down in sections going from top to bottom, left to right. This thing wasn't going anywhere, you couldn't pull it down, you couldn't move it. The columns of the façade were held together by spandrels, plates that provided cross-bracing, in groups of three. We planned to pull the sticks all the way across from north to south, completely burn through two of them, then halfway through on the third one. Then we would attach a cable to one of the grapplers and just pull it over. As Jim Abadie referred to it, we'd "worry" the steel until it falls.

We couldn't pull the steel down on top of the Vista Hotel, though, without collapsing the building down into the basement, which potentially could destroy human remains. But we had a 1,000-ton crane on West Street, one of the biggest cranes in the world. It could have reached over the top of the Marriott hotel and then set the steel onto West Street.

Instead, they decided to take three grapplers, attach cables to the structure and try to pull it down all at once. Griffin, the DDC, almost everyone wanted to do this except me and the ironworkers. We disagreed from day one, but they all thought it would be the fastest way to go, so we agreed to try.

We asked the operators if they were willing to do it, because you can't just ask a guy to hook up a grappler directly to a cable— it's not safe being attached like that, because if the façade falls, the cable attached will pull the machine along with it. We asked the operators, "How do you want to do it?"

They said, "We'll tie the cable to an I-beam and we'll grab the I-beam with the grappler." So, when they were pulling, if at any minute the operator thought he was in danger, he could just open up the jaws and let the I-beam go. That actually happened a couple of times.

For the first pull, on September 25, we didn't preburn any of the steel. They didn't think we needed to. We cleared the surrounding area and from about 150 or 200 feet away the three grapplers backed up simultaneously until the cables were tensioned, then just kept backing up—they didn't use their hydraulics to pull.

They were synchronized. All the operators had radios. They would wait for the signal then they'd back up and get to where the heel of the machines were all up in the air.

It was pretty wild. Believe me, you see a 250,000-pound machine like those grapplers going up on one leg and then coming back down, then going up on two legs and then coming back down . . . I'd be thinking, "Should I stop this guy?" He's determined to take this thing down no matter what happens. Then his cable would snap and we'd say, "Thank God his cable snapped," because that guy was going to go until the cable snapped. That was a milestone in their life for these guys, to do that with a machine.

But it wasn't enough to cause enough stress on the spandrels to snap them. We pulled on those things for like three days until we finally got them to give a little.

Over the course of those three days, September 25 to September 27, during which time the ironworkers were finally allowed to precut some of the sections to weaken them, one seven-story section of the façade finally tore loose and came crashing down. Workers at the site cheered when it fell, but in retrospect, for all the drama, it was an empty victory: it was impossible to control the falling steel during the pull-down, and the impact was far more violent than anyone had foreseen.

CHARLIE VITCHERS

The ironworkers had the right idea. It was going to take a little more time, but what was the hurry? Everybody clapped when that one piece finally came down, but you know what? They couldn't do the rest of it.

BOBBY GRAY

I cheered when that first section came down because I wasn't really paying much attention to engineering at that point. In hindsight it was a foolish thing to do, a very foolish thing to do. It did more damage below than anything else could have.

RICHARD GARLOCK, ENGINEER

I fought tooth and nail against the South Tower pull-down. Not just that it was being pulled down rather than given a haircut, but because of the direction it was being pulled. They pulled it down away from the footprint of the Tower, which was well compacted with debris, and brought it down on top of below-grade structures that were still intact and providing bracing of the slurry wall. I'm not saying I had the only handle on that, but I had an opinion and I knew the pull-down would cause the below-grade structure to become more unstable. I disagreed with the method. I argued my case and lost.

When a 20- to 30-ton portion of the façade finally fell, it came crashing down on the edge of the site on Liberty Street. Within days, it would become clear that the pull-down had caused tremendous damage. At that point, Charlie, Bobby, Sam, and others began to wonder when the DDC would give the okay for the ironworkers to take the façades down piece by piece.

But a different plan was already in the works.

RICHARD GARLOCK, ENGINEER

What we began to hear next was talk about bringing in helicopters . . . that the wash from the blades was going to knock down the façades! When I heard that I thought, "You've got to be kidding. How did they think those columns were still standing after having a 110-story building come down around them?" The connections between the columns and spandrels were still intact. There was structure holding them up.

CHARLIE VITCHERS

When one of those demo guys said, "The oscillation of the wind" from helicopters would knock those fucking things down, I got up and walked out of the meeting. We'd been pulling and pulling on this thing with grapplers. There was no way a helicopter was going to come and knock that thing down.

There was no science to pulling it down; it was common sense. It needed to come down one spandrel, one panel, one column at a time, cutting through the connections. In the time we spent trying to pull, we probably could have given that thing a haircut and had it down.

In the end, of course, we cut it down, piece by piece. We were able to control where it was going and how it was going to fall. We had the blueprints of the façade and I would sit there with one of the demo guys, and we would decide where we were going to cut and drop. We would give the prints to the ironworkers, go over that with them, they would go up in a man basket and they would do what we asked them to do.

There was no concern that we'd accidentally knock the rest of the façade down. That's how strong they were. The bottom of these crucibles were box beams. Eventually we cut them like you would a tree, on a wedge so that they couldn't tip back. We'd leave a little stick in there, then we'd hook the cable up and just pull it away. Everything was taken out in controlled increments.

We could have even left the façade up and dug everything out down to grade below it. They should have. How could you get a better memorial? If we couldn't pull it down, it wasn't coming down on its own.

BOBBY GRAY

I guess at some point in time they realized that dropping the stuff on the slurry wall was not a good idea.

The World Trade Center was built on reclaimed land. As far back as the late 1700s, men had dumped fill into the Hudson River to expand the dimensions of the southern tip of Manhattan. Over the centuries, all manner of debris had been used for this purpose, pushing the shoreline more than 200 yards to the west.

But there was a problem. Water always finds its own level and, despite the millions of yards of material that had been used to create this new land, the waters of the Hudson were always striving to return.

Before the Trade Center could even be built, the problem of water had to be overcome. Long before excavation could begin, engineers had to find a way to excavate an enormous hole—70 feet below grade—without having it fill with water. Simple pumping was not a solution—water pressure from outside the hole would have caused the walls of the pit to cave in as soon as it was excavated. Moreover, the hole had to be kept dry and stable not only during construction, but during the life of the Trade Center.

The solution was a slurry wall. Before the excavation began, a deep trench, reaching down to bedrock, was dug around the entire site. This trench was filled with a man-made mud called bentonite—slurry—which is denser than the surrounding soil and would keep the trench walls from collapsing. Once the slurry was in place, 155 panel-shaped boxes of steel reinforcing bars, welded and wired together in a grid pattern, were lowered into the trench by crane. Concrete was poured onto the steel-paneled boxes, ultimately displacing the slurry.

The result was an impervious wall 3 feet thick and 3,294 feet in circumference that paralleled the south side of Vesey Street, the east side of West Street, and the north side of Liberty Street, then ran north on the west side of the 1 and 9 subway lines, roughly alongside what had once been Greenwich Street, back up to Vesey.

Once the wall was complete, earth from the interior was removed. Holes were drilled through the wall, outward and down, 35 feet into the surrounding bedrock. Massive bundles of steel cables, called tiebacks, were inserted into these holes and bound to the bedrock with grout. The end result created a bathtub of sorts—a container that protected the site from the waters of the Hudson.

The tiebacks were not to be permanent. They gave the site the security it needed while the permanent protection against the Hudson River was built within the bathtub itself. This was a subterranean grid of structural steel and concrete that stretched from one side of the slurry wall to the opposite side, forming the six subterranean levels of the World Trade Center. This sub-grade structure braced the slurry wall from within and made the tiebacks redundant. Once the structure was complete, the tiebacks were then cut so construction could take place around the Trade Center.

Both of the Twin Towers, the Vista Hotel, and Building Six resided within the slurry wall. When they collapsed, millions of pounds of debris fell with enough force to be registered on local seismographs. Within hours, engineers familiar with the Trade Center feared that the collapse of the Towers had crushed or otherwise compromised vast portions of the interior steel structure and the concrete slabs that braced the slurry wall. Among those engineers familiar with the structure, there was deep apprehension that at least some portions of the slurry wall were without this interior support. They feared that the wall was being held up only by the massive debris pile. If the walls failed, the result would be a slow but still catastrophic flood that would fill the site with water.

Soon after the collapse, George Tamaro, the engineer who supervised the original construction of the slurry wall, made the DDC aware of the issue. He warned against allowing heavy machinery to breach the wall, advising that such equipment move around the site with caution.

Although the crane operators knew they were responsible for the safety of themselves and their machines and were generally cautious anyway—in most cases they would not set up their machines on the street without considering the presence of watermains and other underground structures—the work on the pile compelled them to take risks they'd have never attempted elsewhere.

A full assessment of the wall's integrity was not immediately possible because the engineers couldn't get deep enough into the pile to do the necessary reconnaissance. Anecdotal evidence suggested that, for the time being, the wall was sound, held in place by debris even where the below-grade structure was compromised. Work on the pile continued.

But Peter Rinaldi, Richard Garlock, and other engineers wanted proof, and they refocused their efforts on exploring and mapping the condition of the underground levels to ascertain if, in fact, the wall was sound. Only then would they know definitively whether or not a collapse was imminent.

The integrity of the slurry wall was critical. If the wall was compromised and couldn't be made secure, the recovery of victims would be all but impossible.

CHARLIE VITCHERS

Bovis was working the southwest quad. Our assignment was from the Winter Garden south to Battery Park. It probably took us a week and a half to clear off West Street and get most of Liberty Street cleared so we could get around the Vista Hotel. Around the end of September, I started to hear things like, "Well, you're going to be at the slurry wall soon."

And I was like, "What slurry wall?"

I knew what a slurry wall was, but I was thinking, "What does that mean *here*?"

It was only then that I found out that the whole site was surrounded by a slurry wall. That was the very first I had heard of it, and I only found out because I was reviewing some of the drawings that I had gotten from the engineers of a foundation plan of all the levels of the entire site.

The drawings referred to a "slurry wall" just about everywhere.

I didn't realize the importance of the wall in terms of the stability of it until we started thinking about bringing cranes in closer to the pile. I had conversations with Peter Rinaldi and George Tamaro, and I was getting more involved with those meetings happening over at IS 89. I was told, "Charlie, we could have problems with putting cranes up to the edge of the slurry wall because we don't know what the stability is."

Then the operators started asking, "Well, how close can we get to the wall?" So the engineers went to work. They started to organize the placement of the construction equipment that we had down there and tell us what we could do with it. Now I had to go back to the trades and break the bad news to them. These guys had already been digging for a couple weeks and they wanted to keep going down to the bedrock as fast as they could. Now I've got design criteria and have to tell emergency services, the fire department, and the cops, "You guys can't dig over here."

When the slurry wall became a consideration, a lot of people's ears perked up, a lot of people's eyes rolled, and people took a deep breath and said, "Well, what can we do?" The firemen were particularly concerned because they wanted to recover bodies and they realized this was going to affect that. That's when the plans really started to come out. Once the engineers got fully involved and were producing drawings, we had to adhere to them. Nobody really disputed that. We didn't want anybody else getting killed. Because if we had just let people empty that pit, we were told we might have a hole filled with water right now. That was the bottom line. It would be the biggest swimming pool in Manhattan.

PETER RINALDI, PORT AUTHORITY, ENGINEER

My background is in civil engineering. In 2001, I was an engineering program manager for the Port Authority, managing engineering efforts for our tunnels and bridges. But some of my technical training is in what we call the geo-technical foundations of subsurface engineering.

Mike Burton, who was running this with the DDC, knew we needed to focus on this whole underground area and the slurry wall. There was a concern about that collapsing.

The DDC was looking for some help in managing a program on the engineering and logistics of the slurry wall issue and for someone to concentrate on assessing conditions within the site belowground. I had been involved in the reconstruction after the 1993 bombing, so while I wasn't a technical expert on the issue, I had enough technical knowledge and management experience to be useful.

Ray Finnegan, our construction manager at the time, called me up and said I was going to be assigned to the site and to attend the first meeting to discuss the underground area and the slurry wall.

No one knew the condition of the whole underground complex that supported this wall. There was a fear at the time of the wall collapsing. We weren't sure if debris was holding up the wall. There was water leaking into the PATH tubes—the commuter train from New Jersey that ran under the site. The tunnels were flooded, and the pumps couldn't keep up. At first we weren't sure if water was coming in through breaks in the wall or what.

If you actually go back to pre-Colonial times, the Hudson River shoreline ran right along where the eastern-most edge of the slurry wall was, almost down the middle of the site. Over the years, the area was filled in by the Dutch and others. By the 1960s, when the Trade Center was being planned, the shoreline had been pushed several hundred feet farther back along West Street. During construction of the Trade Center, the shoreline was pushed out even farther. The material that was excavated from the World Trade Center site was used in the landfill process that created Battery Park City.

Of the sixteen-acre Trade Center site, roughly eleven acres were surrounded by the slurry wall. I focused on trying to get a team together to brainstorm about how we were going to handle the whole below-grade effort and still support the recovery effort.

We set up a weekly meeting. Initially the focus was highly technical. We figured we were going to have to do tiebacks again. We knew we might have to stabilize the wall and discussed de-watering and putting in wells to remove the water outside the walls, thereby relieving the pressure pushing in on the wall. We started to outline a plan of some of the immediate measures we would take. We also tried to map and get information on the whole underground complex that existed. This was all happening the first two weeks that I was there, from late September into early October.

We were looking to see what condition the wall was in. Was it leaking? Was it broken? Was it supported? Was it unsupported? Where was water coming in? We did that kind of condition assessment.

RICHARD GARLOCK, ENGINEER

I always tried to make sure there were alternative solutions that took into account all the activities going on. I thought the slurry wall was in good shape and that we were only in danger of compromising it by the way operations were being done. I was a voice for the other side in a lot of slurry wall discussions.

Think back to the 1993 bombing. The slurry wall was being braced to the opposite wall through the slabs and structure of the below-grade level. In 1993 the bomb took out significant areas of the below-grade structure. We had areas of intact slab and structure, areas of debris. At that time, we went down there, we looked, we worked out calculations about how much debris we had, and how we would take it out and put back structure.

Fast-forward to 2001. I think the concern over the slurry wall in the papers became a continuation of the terrorists still affecting us, the horror that continued. It became the issue of the day, and I don't think it deserved to be so prominent and newsworthy. It was just something else we had to deal with. The real issue was we had to recover people in a way that was respectful and expeditious. Of course we had to maintain the stability of the site and the slurry wall—that was true, no matter what. But I wasn't alarmed. We engineer solutions, and that's what I think should have been done.

Engineers knew that at least part of the problem with the slurry wall stemmed from groundwater pressure outside the wall, which was pushing inward. Their hope was that by de-watering—pumping out the groundwater behind the wall and sending it back into the Hudson River through intact groundwater systems—they would be able to avoid taking more dramatic action.

CHARLIE VITCHERS

Water was coming in, but I didn't think it was anything we couldn't handle. The de-watering system started up on October 3. We hired a contractor, Mooretrench, and the guys started drilling. There was a design calling for twenty-seven wells on Liberty Street. They were about eight to twelve feet behind the wall, just pumping water twenty-four hours a day, taking the head pressure of the water away from the backside of the wall.

It was amazing engineering. The pumps went in at different elevations. If you put in three pumps in the same hole or near each other at three different depths, at first you're going to be sucking water from all levels of the ground. After it falls below the height of the top pump, you shut it off. After it falls below the second pump, you shut it off. The third pump, the deepest one, maintains it. That made a lot of sense to me. We started drilling wells, putting in casings, and pumped river water back into the river. Once we took the water out from behind the wall, we kept those pumps running.

Some of the sewers we wanted to use were clogged or impaled or broken. We needed to find outfall locations. Any major city around water has them. They're just a gravity drain line, a big pipe that carries away surface water. In Manhattan, they run to the river and have tide gates so if there's high-tide water it won't come back and flood in.

The initial collapse of the South Tower devastated both Liberty Street and just inside the slurry wall that ran parallel to it. The wall along Liberty Street was in the worst shape because the collapse of the Towers basically took the Vista Hotel down on top of it. The Vista Hotel collapse also impacted the wall on West Street. When the South Tower first collapsed, it took out all the sub-grade parking levels and decks for almost the entire length of Liberty Street and exposed a 180- to 200-foot section of the wall. Support of that wall became a concern when we started to get into the debris pile and dig because the more debris we dug out against that wall, the less there was holding it up.

We didn't know what was intact down below, whether heel blocks were still in place in the foundation itself, which might prevent the wall from kicking out. Without lateral support, we were told, there was a possibility the wall could move, that the lateral bracing of this steel matrix on all the levels of the tub might not be attached to the wall anymore.

PETER RINALDI, PORT AUTHORITY, ENGINEER

We needed to remove the water pressure on the wall. We did that in the two areas where we felt the walls were in the most danger and where the most pressure was: on Liberty Street and on West Street. That was where we found the collapse had been so severe that there was very little support for the walls in those areas. We were putting the wells in when the wall started to fail.

On Monday, October 8, maybe 7 A.M., 7:30 A.M., one of the construction guys came up and said, "A crack opened up behind the wall last night, there's a crack opened up behind the wall here in the street."

I walked down and had a look. Right away I knew that this was what we called a classic failure of the retaining wall. I had seen this before and I was familiar with it. It was an earth-pressure wedge. When the wall starts to move out, a wedge of soil behind it kind of moves with it. I looked at where that crack was and you could see the line opening up in the soil.

"The wall is moving," I said. "That's the only way this could be happening." It was what we had all feared.

I found Mike Burton and I said, "We have a little problem, Mike. It looks like the slurry wall is moving over on Liberty Street." We went running out there and both took a look and tried to figure out what to do. We had surveyors shoot a couple of bench marks and laser marks and we started monitoring it to measure the movements. I remember calling Mike hourly and telling him how much it was moving because he had gotten called in to the mayor's office on this and was in meetings with the mayor.

CHARLIE VITCHERS

In twenty-four hours it went from maybe a six-inch crack to about a twelve-inch crack. There was kind of a panic. I walked over there and looked at it the way I look at everything. And I just made an assessment.

"That's not too bad," I said. "Look at the debris pile inside the wall. It's not moving any farther than that." But there was a big void in there. The engineers couldn't prove that it wasn't going to move any more.

One of the hardest things, emotionally, was when the engineers decided that the slurry wall was compromised. George Tamaro, the original engineer for the construction of the wall back in the 1960s, made the call: "Fill it up with sand." And we did. We put 55,000 cubic yards of sand in the hole. The cops and the firemen were like, "What? Are you out of your fucking mind? We got guys down there. You're burying them."

But the engineers told us that if this thing keeps moving we're gonna have seawater coming in any day.

PETER RINALDI, PORT AUTHORITY, ENGINEER

We could see that from our inspections the wall was unsupported pretty far down. Then the wall obviously started to move. There was always a concern that a catastrophic collapse could happen, that the slurry wall would collapse, that water would inundate the site. The PATH tunnels, which were connected to the site, were plugged on the Jersey side, filled with concrete, just in case.

We could get fill material in on the corner with a frontend loader or a dozer, but in this other area it was all unstable. We were able to get conveyer belts with a long reach and actually reach over the wall, through the slabs and debris, until we were over the area that was hollow underneath. Very quickly we dropped the material down.

When you looked at the wall in terms of that area and location, it really shouldn't have been standing. There was no support for it over a long distance along Liberty Street. That was one of the areas that we identified as critical, and that was the first area we put the tiebacks in.

While the slurry wall along Liberty Street was temporarily stabilized with de-watering and fill, the engineers had reached a consensus to install new tiebacks and reattach the slurry wall to the surrounding bedrock, which would allow the workers to continue to remove debris without compromising the integrity of the wall. At the end of the lengthy process the pit would look much like it did before the Trade Center structure was originally built. The new tieback operation began on October 12.

SAM MELISI, FDNY

Once the slurry wall became an issue, suddenly every individual thing that happened on that site had to take the slurry wall into account. Everything else that was happening on-site was interesting to us, but we would really take notes about the tiebacks and the slurry wall because the placement of the tiebacks would dictate where we were going to be able to search. It was that simple.

To us, it seemed as if the location of the victims didn't take precedence anymore. It was out of our hands. The engineers told us that if the slurry wall was compromised or in danger of being compromised, they would come in with thousands of yards of fill and dump it into the site to reinforce the wall. We couldn't let that happen; it would mean looking through thousands of yards of material and delay our ultimate goal, which was to find victims in a timely fashion.

CHARLIE VITCHERS

We put the responsibility for the construction of the tiebacks under one of the contractors instead of dividing it up into quadrants. It just didn't make sense to do that any other way. Bovis was designated to be the construction manager for the tieback and slurry wall work. Tully was an independent contractor who actually worked through them.

Even though the slurry wall was moving, we were still digging all over the place. We still had four quadrants and there really wasn't one voice. But I knew that the slurry wall was a consideration everywhere and I said, "What do we do?"

The engineers said, "Let's do a no-fly zone a hundred feet inside the slurry wall. From the slurry wall a hundred feet into the site, you can't dig. You can't move anything until we establish what we have to do to put new tiebacks in."

I was the one who had to go out on the pile and tell the operators and the cops and the firemen, "Okay, listen, guys. We can't dig within one hundred feet of the slurry wall. Okay?"

People stared at me like, "Where are you from, fucking Mars? We're digging wherever the hell we want. What, you mean to tell me to get out of here? How can you do that?"

It wasn't just Sam Melisi, it was the general consensus of all the people out in the pit. The fire department had been allowing members of the department who had lost a relative to dig for his son, or dig for his brother. They did not want to stop.

I also had to explain it to the construction workers and equipment operators who were working pretty much for anybody who needed them. I had to go through the chain and produce little logistics drawings for everyone. Everyone would agree, then Sammy would go back and talk to the firemen and say, "Listen, this is serious, guys. We can't work within one hundred feet of the wall. You know Charlie . . . the engineer said one hundred feet but Charlie fought for seventy-five, so we got seventy-five."

That would make it work.

JIM ABADIE, BOVIS

As different tasks started coming up, I kept saying, "Hey, we can take care of that." So Bovis ended up taking on more of the management of the job. I started bringing in different people and started running it like a typical construction site, but obviously with the sensitivity of working for the fire department and helping them and assisting them on doing the recoveries.

We mobilized the tieback rigs and George Tamaro started coming up with a plan. We could attack other stuff while the designs and the plans were being made and the equipment was being maneuvered into place.

There was an area on Liberty Street where we could start experimenting. We got some tieback rigs and figured out where they wanted to drill through the panels.

That was the first area to attack. We had to figure out the logistics of how to put them in. That became the real issue of the tieback installation. It's not the design. We worked out the engineering, but it was really the installation process and how you do that. How do you find the wall? The wall is under this debris. How do you get to it and how do you remove that debris in a way that's safe because that debris is holding up the wall?

Charlie, myself, and Joe Carsky from Tully devised a plan the engineers approved. We decided to hopscotch. We would excavate one area of debris, put a tieback in, then move over maybe 50 feet, and take out another pocket of material and put a tieback in. Later, we would come in between.

The new tiebacks were designed to be temporary. They were designed to be more robust than the original temporary ones, and we designed them to last longer, but they were by no means made to be permanent. These temporary tiebacks would tie the wall back so we would safely be able to remove and search the material, but eventually, as reconstruction of the site goes forward, a permanent structure will have to be put back and the new tiebacks will be cut like the original ones.

CHARLIE VITCHERS

We first had to cut holes in the wall. Then we used hooties to install the tiebacks. Hooties are a self-contained platform about fourteen feet long and six feet wide that run on tracks, like an excavator. Where we could, we would just back them up against the slurry wall. In places, we had to hang them over the wall from a crane. We called those hanging leads. Each unit had a diesel-operated drill mast for drilling the holes, like a big well driller, and a winch head and drum for pulling the pipe and setting the cable into the hole. Then it would be filled with grout to hold it fast to the bedrock and tensioned. Setting each cable was a three-day process. All we had to do was feed them pipe, for water and the air compressor. At any one time we probably had seven hooties working on the site, including backup machines. Danny Mirt of Nicholson was responsible for that operation.

Even though there had been some disagreement over the need to reinstall the tiebacks, the issue had forced the various parties at work in the pit—the contractors, the Port Authority, FDNY, PAPD, the DDC—to come together. For the first time, the need for coordination and cooperation had been underscored and recognized. The threat to the slurry wall had dramatically illustrated the fact that every activity on the site had the potential to affect every other activity. The lesson would not go unnoticed. As the tieback operation got under way, cleanup and recovery efforts continued. Debris was removed alongside portions of the wall, which allowed the new tiebacks to be put in place. Maneuvering around the no-fly zone, workers concentrated their efforts farther into the interior of the pile.

The cut-down of the South Tower shrouds, several weeks earlier, meant that workers in the Bovis and Tully quadrants could create a roadway of compacted debris. This road would allow grapplers and other heavy machines to penetrate deeper into the debris field and allow debris to be trucked out. This road, known as Tully Road, became the primary roadway into and out of the pile.

The construction of the road, however, came with a devastating cost. As long as it was actively in use, it would be impossible to proceed with recovery efforts in the debris directly beneath the road itself.

CHARLIE VITCHERS

We were stuck with the task of deciding, "Okay, where are we going now?" The tieback operation started off on Liberty Street. That was the only wall that had drawings specifying where we could proceed. The engineers were working as fast as they could to produce drawings for West Street, Liberty and Greenwich and Vesey Street, but that took a little bit of time.

Tully was basically developing roads over the whole site without a plan. They wanted to build this big cul-de-sac inside Tower Two and they had another road that just went straight up north. I didn't go for that. I made it coincide with the road we were using, coming in from the west end, because I wanted two roads to meet in the Tower because that was the only safe place to stand on the debris pile without worrying about a void collapsing underneath us.

I went back and developed a plan with no quadrant markings on it. I marked out the roadway path, where the two would meet, and said, "This is the Tully road," and then we had Tully Road. It wasn't a real road that was paved, just a truck route over the debris, with millings, old asphalt, to create a surface on top of it. But we had to move equipment over something.

What was incredible was that as we excavated down alongside the road, we found firemen compressed in the debris way down under the road bed. I remember it like it was yesterday, because we had recoveries going on all over the place that day. It was a day when it just wouldn't stop—one of many days that I don't remember it stopping. One hit after another. Everywhere I looked there was another recovery going on, another body. The cops had somebody, four fire department battalions had somebody, and then they find this guy under the road. They saw a bunker jacket.

By the time I got there, the firemen already had a burner and an ironworker and a laborer and a backhoe operator there trying to clear out debris so they could get him, cutting steel here, clawing at debris there. But the operator realized he was undermining the road, that if he removed any more debris it was going to come crashing down. So he stopped. Sam Melisi called me down and showed me where the guy was, and showed me the guy's jacket, and I was like, "Oh boy."

This was way down below the surface of the road, twenty, thirty feet at least.

We first had an ironworker cut a piece of one of the big spandrels and burn a notch out in the steel and we shoved it in there ten feet above this whole operation so at least nothing else would fall down. Then we got the engineers over there. They kept saying, "You really shouldn't. You really shouldn't. You really shouldn't." They were afraid we were going to compromise the road.

That was the big problem: "Can we get this guy out without fucking up the road?"

The engineers determined that we couldn't get the guy out without the possibility of undermining the road. And if we did that, we'd be stuck with no way to get anybody out.

RICHARD GARLOCK, ENGINEER

I remember that recovery distinctly. At that point, after backfilling had been used to support the slurry wall on Liberty Street, it had become the de facto solution to structure and debris collapse everywhere. The attitude was, "If you have a problem, backfill."

By this point I had a very good relationship with the fire department and the contractors. I sat with Sam and Charlie and explained that even though I disagreed, backfilling had become the solution. I told them if they undermined Tully Road it would cause a backfilling operation, which would cover up everything. I asked, from their viewpoint, to understand, because if the road was undermined, there would be more fill dumped on top of those firemen, which would have delayed their recovery and made it even more difficult.

CHARLIE VITCHERS

We eventually had to pour sand in to stabilize the road, and re-dig it out again. They called a woman down from the medical examiner's office and brought her over to the body. She spent about two hours there and finally she determined it wasn't one person, it was two people.

I told Sammy, "Listen, you guys do what you gotta do. You need an ironworker? You need laborers? Just let me know what you're gonna do." And then I left. I just walked away. We told the operators just keep going. We all looked the other way and let them do what they liked.

And that's what they did. The guys were very flat about it, deadpan. They didn't say a word. They wanted to get these guys out.

The next morning I came in and they had the guys out. The firemen had literally gone in there and dug a big cave under the road. I grabbed a couple of ironworkers and I had the grappler operator get some steel beams and I said, "Start welding some sticks back into that hole. In case the debris collapses, maybe we'll catch it."

We kind of just buried that one under the rug. Everybody was satisfied. I even think the engineers just looked the other way.

I realized each person's position. I could understand how the firemen felt, because they had two of their guys, but they don't know who. Now they could open up their jacket, find a badge or something, and know who they got. Because they couldn't go to bed at night knowing they were leaving someone there, so they couldn't leave them there. They could not do that. I could not have done that. If that was my kid, I'd be down there with a torch myself saying, "Fuck you," to everybody, "I'm getting him out."

Next morning, they were out. Two more guys found.

CHAPTER SIX

THE TRAILER

The general superintendent has to know. *That's the job.*

The chain of command on a construction site is clear. At the top sits the general super. Authority then flows through him to the subcontractor supervisors and foremen and from them to the tradesmen in the field. The general superintendent is responsible for everything *on-site—budget management, long-range planning, logistics, scheduling, safety, machinery, personnel. A project manager and other staff provide administrative support, but the general super has to make sure that everyone knows what to do at every moment.*

With a tight, top-down management hierarchy comes focused coordination of the entire construction site. The crane operators, electricians, plumbers, and other tradesmen all work together with the complete confidence that they are doing the one essential task within their specialty to move the job forward. They know that they will not be endangering other workers; nor will they themselves be endangered. They need not worry where they are going to get their materials or whether they'll run out of gas or that the electricity will be turned off midday. They know that when the concrete trucks start rolling up to begin a pour, the rebar and formwork will be ready. And they never need to worry that they might, at any time, be broadsided by a grappler.

They know all these things because at normal construction sites, one single person—the general superintendent—calls the shots. He knows what everybody is doing and where they're doing it, because they are following his directions. Day to day, hour to hour, the workers know that their general super has got it covered.

Not so at Ground Zero. Not yet.

While the quad system provided rudimentary order, by mid-October there was still no recognized logistics map, chain of command, or central organization. Except for the work being done on the slurry wall, each of the four major contractors continued to work independently, all but oblivious to the work going on in the quadrant next to them. The long-range planning and logistical coordination, provided at daily meetings by the DDC, were woefully inadequate and focused on timetables, procedural concerns, and political considerations—rarely on anything that would directly facilitate work on the pile.

BOBBY GRAY

I was going to meetings any place just to get information; anytime I heard there was a meeting I tried to get to it. I was going to some of the DDC meetings at IS 89. A lot of times I would come out worse than when I went in—I would actually have less information. I'm not a bureaucrat, I don't work well with bureaucracy, and that's all that I was hearing, bureaucratic concerns.

The powers-that-be would present their ideas, but without too much thought about how to do it. They were telling people to move machines on the pile from A to B, but they weren't looking at what it took to do that. They didn't know how to get machines from A to B. I know they felt a responsibility—they wanted to do it the right way because it was all on them. But they were money handlers.

You had to be in the pit to really understand what the contractors and recovery workers were doing every day.

CHARLIE VITCHERS

Basically, what the DDC normally does is observe and report. On a normal project they walk the site with the contractor to make sure equipment they are paying for is on-site and that man counts are correct, because they answer to the city. At Ground Zero I'm sure that was more complicated because they had to answer to FEMA and every other agency involved. But in the real world the DDC doesn't really have a role in logistics or scheduling activities on the job.

Normally, the DDC has hundreds of jobs going on simultaneously in New York City—a school here, a firehouse here, a hospital there—with different contractors in charge of each one who coordinate all activities and make sure everything is done safely. But they are all separate jobs with nothing in common. On this job *everything* was in common, but with different contractors running different parts of it, so the DDC couldn't treat it the way they treated a normal job. You couldn't do it like that. Somebody was going to get killed, somebody was going to get hurt. A lot of people in all the agencies down there, contractors and uniformed personnel, had problems understanding what was expected of them. People were frustrated because they didn't have any authority to dictate to somebody else what should be done.

BOBBY GRAY

To me, because there was no coordination, the result looked like a land grab between quadrant contractors and subcontractors. It pissed me off that this was even allowed to happen. I could understand it if this was a situation where two buildings were going up at the same time. A smart contractor with two buildings going up hires two different subs and promises a $100,000 bonus to whoever gets to the top first—it's a no-brainer.

This was not that. This was something else entirely. It looked like the more land you could grab, the more time you would be there, and the more money you would make. Contractors got paid per machine and operator, so if one contractor had ten machines working they made more money than the contractor that had six machines working. They were making this more of a business than a recovery.

But we were not there for that. To me, this job was about recovery. But I wasn't handing out the checks to pay for the whole thing either. I looked at it way more emotionally than the guys writing the checks because I was there from September 11 on. At points it looked to me like the DDC was only concerned with trying to get this thing done, get the pile down to street level, before Giuliani left office at the end of the year.

It started to smell like politics and business, people wanting to make money. In reality, I guess that was a big part of why some people were there. At some level the contractors were there to make money and we got paid too, so I'm as guilty of that as anybody. But to me it was just never a business.

What the DDC wanted wasn't necessarily gonna happen because it wasn't practical in the field. The DDC was just sitting down and just screaming at the contractors, but there was no buffer. I can tell you what I think a machine can do, but that's it. So in the meantime the contractors were trying to do what the DDC was telling them, and going where they wanted them to go, and it became a land grab. Contractors were trying to get as much of the site as they could, get their machines as far into an area as possible, and having my people, the operating engineers, doing crazy stuff, not working safe. I'd see Joe Operator way over there and think, "Why is he all the way over there?" And then I'd realize, "Oh, that's the edge of Tully's zone and he's trying to get into Grace's area." That part was ugly. Grapplers were falling through the floors and all kinds of stuff like that was going on.

For example, the DDC would say they wanted the Vista Hotel down. So one contractor would say, "We're gonna get two machines on the top of the Vista Hotel and we're gonna start taking down the east wall of the Vista."

No one was saying, "Look, we sent engineers in and assessed it. You really should come up this way, and if you tear this down, this may fall."

No one was saying, "Let's back up, tighten up the laces, figure it out, and then we'll go ahead."

No. It was just, "We're gonna do this and we're gonna do that, we're gonna go over here and we're gonna build a road there."

Public servants were acting like construction experts. I always resented that. They had no field experience, no practical experience in trying to do what they were trying to do. It was chaotic at best. There was no rhyme or reason for what was going on.

As far as the DDC was concerned, it was, "Do it my way or the highway."

Those contractors on the pile were in a position few had ever been in before. With no one acting as a general superintendent between the contractors and the DDC, work in the separate quadrants was frequently at odds with what was happening fifty feet away. There was no mechanism in place to coordinate activities or arbitrate disputes. On the pile, no one was in charge because everyone was in charge, and everyone was in charge because no one told them they were not.

CHARLIE VITCHERS

There was a big turf war there for a while between the contractors. The South Tower, Tower Two, was in our quadrant and I remember begging Tully, "Can you please let me just get two pieces of equipment inside Tower Two?" I had to remove debris in a safe and controlled way to expose steel behind the Vista Hotel so we could cut down some spears. But Tully had moved their line to within the inside edge of the Tower. They were inside hacking at the spears from the other side. We were on the outside, sixty feet below them, and it was dangerous.

Grace, one of our subcontractors, had some grapplers up there. He's reaching up into the pile inside the Tower and Tully's guys are in the Tower. They were pulling stuff back their way as fast as they could and Grace was trying to pull stuff their way as fast as they could. It was like the standoff at the OK Corral.

We thought we'd be able to get in when Tully brought their equipment out for maintenance, but they never brought their equipment out; it all stayed right there. I finally went up there with a roll of yellow caution tape and I said, "Give me twenty-five feet inside the Tower so we can safely work on the spears on the outside." I pulled the caution tape all the way across the pit on that smoking, frickin' pile, tied it around one of the box beams, and it melted on me.

I finally talked to their operators individually, I said, "Listen, guys, we just need you guys to work safe." So they stayed back.

Then I had to convince Jimmy Tully to let me take two of our machines through "Tully territory," so we could daisy-chain debris out and pass it down. Jimmy Tully says, "You can have *one* machine."

All right, well, one's better than none, so I got one machine up there but one of Tully's operators wasn't into the game plan. He picked up this box beam, rolls it—*BOOM*—and blocks our operator from coming through.

I was waiting for our operator to grab one end and the other guy to grab the other and have a tug-of-war. I'm like, "Are you guys in the same union, or what?" We finally worked that out and got him in and by the next morning we had two machines up on the back of the hill. Jimmy came up to me and he goes, "You know, give you a fucking inch and you take a goddamn mile."

"You're right," I said, "but our machinery has to be working safe."

Two days later we found the antenna from Tower One in the footprint of Tower Two, in that twenty-five-foot section of ours. Port Authority wanted to save that as an artifact so we had to work with a crane reaching into Tower Two and we slowly pushed Tully back.

It was wild. Head games.

BOBBY GRAY

We temporarily lost a recovery over that kind of stuff, on the north end of the Vista. Because of my experience in rigging, Sam Melisi asked me, "Can you help me down here? We're trying to box out this area where we have a recovery."

My guys and I crawled in and got box beams to protect where this guy was buried, so no matter what some asshole did above us, at least that body would be protected. It was really too dangerous for anybody to be in there—even I didn't want to be in there.

But when the shift changed that night, so did the attitude. I came back the next day and the box beams were gone. The guy was reburied. That was due to the confusion of the situation. I didn't even know whose quad it was.

• • •

At Ground Zero, the DDC assumed the role of the building or property owner on a normal job. But they had no general superintendent equivalent to translate their mandates and goals to the reality on the ground. To the workers, it often appeared that the DDC was only interested in pushing everyone to work faster, with little consideration for the impact that speed had on the recovery process. The faster and cheaper the work was done, the better the DDC would look. Rough estimates made as early as September speculated that the job would take as long as three years and cost as much as $3 billion, but that was only a guess. As a result, the DDC applied constant pressure to remove more and more material from the site ever faster. Deputy Commissioner Michael Burton wanted to have the site down to street level by the end of New York mayor Rudolph Giuliani's term, a goal he intended to meet.

That aspiration, however, was not shared by the vast majority of the men and women working on the pile. They saw the job in a radically different way: to them, it was all about recovery. Day after day, they were removing bodies and body parts, hardly an experience any of them wanted to extend, but one they considered a sacred responsibility. The removal of debris was incidental and they bristled at demands that treated the presence of dead human beings as an unwelcome distraction or an impediment to speed, financial efficiency, or political gain.

The construction workers—already under tremendous emotional pressure and battling physical fatigue—bore the burden of the resulting inefficiency. Morale, already problematic due to the relentless specter of human remains, sagged. By mid-October, the crisis was reaching a tipping point. They were afraid someone was going to get killed.

The solution to the quandary of organizational turmoil evolved out of one of the small trailers that sat on the fringes of Ground Zero. Identical to those trailers that sit on every construction site, it served as office space for job supervisors, a quiet place to make a phone call, do paperwork, con-

sult architectural and engineering plans, hold a brief meeting. On most job sites what takes place in such trailers is as spare and utilitarian as the architecture of the structure itself.

Again, at Ground Zero, this would not be the case. The activities in one particular trailer became extraordinarily important.

From the very beginning, Jim Abadie and other Bovis personnel had been holding mandatory morning and evening meetings in their small trailer just outside the loading dock of One World Financial. In October, one man—the newly named daytime superintendent of Bovis—would step forward to assume leadership. He turned that trailer into a command center, a place where contractors, engineers, union representatives, and, eventually, FDNY, PAPD, and other agencies would come together and slowly but surely—and informally—begin to bring order to the chaos of the pile.

That man was Charlie Vitchers.

CHARLIE VITCHERS

The first Bovis trailer on Albany Street was just a little 8 by 15-foot trailer with a little desk set up in it that we brought in while we were still working out of the One World Financial Center loading dock. After about a week, we brought in another 8 by 30-foot foot trailer—an empty trailer like a mobile home with paneling on the walls—for meetings with our own staff of supervisors and foremen, and the subcontractors working for us, like the labor foreman and the carpenter foreman.

We had the carpenters make up some benches and some big tables. I put plastic laminate over them so I could slide the drawings of the site under them so our people could get familiar with it. On the walls we put up a couple of drawings of the site, whatever we had, hung American flags all over the place. It was very patriotic.

Jim Abadie ran those meetings every day at the same time, at 7 in the morning and at 5:30 P.M. If we needed meetings in between that, we'd meet individually. Those meetings were mandatory for our staff. I don't think the DDC and other government agencies had any idea how organized we were, that we were already having meetings that were making sense and planning the logistics of the site twice a day. The other contractors were flying by the seat of their pants, still trying to get their own trailers set up.

JIM ABADIE, BOVIS

Bovis started taking on different tasks beyond just removing the debris and trucking it out. We had gotten involved in putting in the de-watering system to try to keep the water level down and we got involved with the tieback system. We got involved doing all these different logistics plans. So we started becoming the focal point for a lot of activity on the site. People started coming to our meetings so they could get the overview of where we were. AMEC would be there, Tully would be there, and they would tell us what they were gonna do. We started getting a lead role, I guess, because I was sitting there with Mike Burton in the very beginning, trying to advise him. Some of it is just being in the right place at the right time.

The DDC soon recognized that Bovis was adept at doing precisely what the DDC was not: tracking and coordinating personnel, materials, and machinery on a vast scale. As a construction management company already familiar with the DDC and their administrative needs, Bovis was quickly able to transfer office personnel and managers to the site and manage the growing amount of resources coming in.

CHARLIE VITCHERS

Jim Abadie got together all the construction companies that were down there, including the subcontractors, dozens and dozens of them. He went to the DDC and said, "Listen, let us handle all of the ironworkers, let us handle this and that." The work in our quadrant became more efficient. The shock and the initial panic was over. We needed organization, because just because somebody has a torch doesn't mean he should be out there burning steel. When we first got everybody together in the trailer, the organization started coming together without somebody from the administrative level to come down out of the IS 89 and say, "This is what we want." Everybody who was at the trailer already had an assignment to do. We were making decisions.

The DDC ran meetings at IS 89 at 9 A.M. and 4 P.M. for all the head honchos, company presidents and guys like that. Jim Abadie was going to those meetings the first couple of weeks and then coming back and talking to me and the guys, telling us, "This is what was discussed, this is what's important." All the things that concerned the DDC. At some point, Jim said, "Charlie, why don't you start coming up to these meetings with me?"

So I went up there with him. Michael Burton, the deputy commissioner of the DDC, ran those meetings. But they couldn't cover everything, and there was almost no involvement and input from people who were working on-site, no communication, none at all. A lot of things that the DDC was concerned about, like the administrative end of the job, the money, or brainstorming about how they were going to close off the perimeters of the site, didn't really help us on the pile.

At the Bovis trailer, we had a room full of foremen who wanted to go out and work, not a room full of guys that wanted to brainstorm. That was the difference between the meetings.

So I'd leave the DDC meeting, go down to the trailer, and have a foreman's meeting and explain to our people, "Here's what we're doing today, here's what we're doing tomorrow, here's what we want to do after that."

The fact that Bovis was having regular meetings to discuss site logistics and planning was, for many of the key people on-site, a breakthrough. It was the only place on the whole site, apart from impromptu bitch sessions held by disgruntled workers, where there was even an attempt to talk about the job as a whole and look ahead.

Word about the meetings traveled fast on the pile. Soon, union representatives and the supervisors of the other quadrants began drifting in to the meetings to pick up information that they could pass on to their own workers. At first, this small group rarely numbered more than two dozen.

What they heard in the trailer was a revelation. It couldn't have been more different from the DDC meetings. Instead of screaming, there was calm. Instead of voices talking over one another, there was discussion. Instead of conflict, there was consensus. No one held back. Charlie Vitchers was stepping up, speaking out, making sense, and being heard. He wasn't assigned to do this, he just did it. Eventually, even the DDC began to listen.

BOBBY GRAY

I only heard about Bovis's trailer meetings through word of mouth, probably in the last week of September. Somebody told me, "Hey, they're trying to get something together. A game plan is being formatted, you've got to go to this meeting." The Bovis trailer, from my perspective, was always important because that's where I got my details, that's what really evolved into "the trailer."

I remember the first meeting I went to there, in the little trailer on Albany Street. Charlie really hadn't emerged yet, but I met Lou Mendes, who was an assistant to Michael Burton with the DDC. They were trying to lay out, for lack of better words, a battle plan. I needed to know that because I needed to figure out how many pieces of equipment they were going to need, what was gonna stay and what wasn't gonna stay, and, if they wanted my input, what I was thinking would work and what wouldn't.

The whole site was just chaotic at the time, working but chaotic. Out on the pile, we all knew it couldn't go on like this, that at some point that wasn't gonna work anymore. Everybody had their own idea about what they wanted to do, but no one really seemed to have a plan of attack.

CHARLIE VITCHERS

Lou Mendes of the DDC finally got smart and said to one of his soldiers, "I want one of you guys to go to the Bovis meetings in the morning and in the afternoon, and just sit there and find out what's going on." Our meetings were still very informal, just a conversation that sometimes lasted twenty minutes and sometimes lasted two hours.

Then after a couple of days Lou Mendes started to follow me after the DDC meeting back down to the Bovis trailer, to make sure that we were on the same page. But he would come in and start screaming at everybody, call everybody an idiot. "You guys don't know what the fuck you're doing! Why's it taking so long to do this, why's it taking so long to do that?"

I'd come in the morning and Lou would say, "I thought I told you to tell these guys to do A, B, and C last night; they only did A, what the fuck is wrong with you, can't you get the word across to these guys?" He belittled a lot of people, and some people got gun shy about speaking out.

I'd go, "Lou, we had recoveries last night. We couldn't do B and C." But I didn't hold Lou at fault for anything. He wanted to have his finger on everything. Lou was smart in that sense and I understood his intentions were good. Like everyone else, he was very emotional because of what was going on, and I knew that he had to answer to the higher authorities, Mike Burton of the DDC and the mayor's office.

I started a sign-in sheet at the meetings so I would be able to track who the regulars were. The sign-in sheet actually made people feel like they had a formal presence, because nobody on this job site was making anybody sign in at a meeting. All we had were conversations, but with no proof that they took place. Just the fact that we made people sign in was a good thing because it showed they wanted to take responsibility. The same guys from the DDC and the trades would show up. At first that was ourselves—Bovis, Koch, and the ironworkers, Grace and Gateway and the demo contractors. It evolved from there. Jimmy Tully would show up or one of his supervisors. Same thing with AMEC. Somebody would be there from DH Griffin. Then all of a sudden guys like Sam Melisi of the fire department were asking, "Oh, you guys are having a meeting? When are your meetings?"

I told him, "Yeah, we're having a meeting, Sam. They're at 7 A.M. and 5:30 P.M. You're welcome to come. Anything you need?"

Sammy came in the next day. That was great. Now we had the fire department in there—let's all talk about what we all need.

SAM MELISI, FDNY

When they started getting the construction crews into that trailer, that established some type of order, some idea of what's going to happen. Those meetings were totally different than the meetings with DDC and the fire department, or the police. At first there was no representation of the uniformed members in the trailer, there was hardly anyone there. We'd just walk in and stand in the back. It wasn't our meeting but we would listen and if we had a lighting issue or something, we would say something. And they would say, "Oh yeah, whatever you need, man." The construction crews were more than gracious to help our needs, to work with us. We were able to bring back some good information from these things and I remember telling some of the other agencies, "These meetings are going on. Send a representative, you know, because it's important."

When the contractors would have a problem, they would ask us, "Hey, what do you know about this?" If we knew about it, we told them; if we didn't, we'd get some information. That's basically how it started. Before, they would see your face out there, they would know you were from the fire department, but they wouldn't really know who you were. Now they did. That's how this kind of working relationship started. It started getting so much more coordinated.

BOBBY GRAY

My relationship with Charlie really started in the trailer meetings. We didn't know each other before September 11, and for the first few weeks down there, he was just another face. But he started speaking out at these meetings. Common sense. People from DDC are saying, "No, we got to be in there, we got to do this," and taking salt shakers and moving them around on a map on the table. But Charlie wasn't just rushing into things. He was actually formulating ideas. He was saying, "Okay, that's great, you want to get a machine here to do this. I think we need to do A, B, and C to get there."

Charlie seemed to be the voice of reason. He was the only guy who made sense to me. I was hoping he would take more control.

CHARLIE VITCHERS

Bobby was a cool cat down there. He was at every meeting, did whatever he was asked to do, and he had a lot of work on his plate. If you needed any kind of Local 14 operating engineers, or needed cranes moved, you went to Bobby and Bobby made sure you had it. He was the go-to guy.

If you needed to know what kind of equipment could handle a certain piece of steel or debris under certain conditions, you got a hold of Bobby. You'd say to him, "I need to reach one hundred and seventy-five feet and I want to try to pick up thirty tons, what can I use for that?" And Bobby could shoot that right off the top of his head. He'd tell you what you could use, but he'd say, "I'm not an engineer, you know," but at least you'd get the piece of equipment you needed from him. Then you'd go to a crane engineer and say, "Give me the details on a triple-8." They'd fax you over the criteria of what that machine is capable of. Then I'd say to Bobby, "All right, let's get that triple-8 over there, I need it over there by seven in the morning." That was his job, and he took care of it. He put the right guy in the right position with the right equipment to do the right job.

He did that for the whole site. At one time we had more than thirty cranes on the job. Bobby was accountable for all those guys, letting them know what their shifts were, the risks, the hazards. He had to check the certification on every machine because some machines hadn't been certified as safe since the last job. You wouldn't know if there was a crack in a boom or a light out. Bobby had to make sure that everything being used down there was safe for the operator to be on, from the tires to the lights to the booms to the hydraulic hoses. He also had to make sure that the guys were qualified operators, that their union cards and licenses were up to date, because if anything bad ever happens, the contractor is liable. Bobby had a lot of responsibility down there, and because he had to bounce around the whole site, he'd pick up things. He was always able to come into a meeting and add something that he saw or make a suggestion that we should do something about this or that, information that generated activity for a lot of other people.

BOBBY GRAY

I've worked my whole life, but operating a crane wasn't something I thought I was going to do.

I was born in 1955 and grew up in Yonkers, very middle class, in an Irish Catholic family. After high school, I went to college for a year then took a year off and just kind of headed west. I washed dishes in a roadside diner and did a lot of skiing in Colorado, but after a year I came back home, went back to school, and became a biology major. I also took an on-campus job in the maintenance department. They had some equipment—little excavators and snow plows. Soon, I was working more than I was going to class. It just seemed natural.

I wouldn't sit in the cafeteria with the other students; I'd sit in the staff dining room because I was more comfortable with the people who worked at the school than I was with the students.

Then, in my junior year, came Comparative Vertebrate Anatomy. That was it. That was the wall, the twenty-fifth mile. I said, "I do not want to know the structure of frogs."

There went my dreams of med school. I left school after my junior year.

My first construction job was working with the guys they call sandhogs, the tunnel workers who build New York City's water tunnels and other underground infrastructure. New York's been building water tunnels for fifty years. They still are. This job was about 800 feet belowground.

Here I was, this kid who thought he was so worldly, working underground with the sandhogs. We'd take a mine hoist down to this cavernous area at the bottom of the shaft, then ride a train to the heading, the farthest point you can get underground in the tunnel. The operating engineers ran all the heavy machinery, from the concrete plant to the mine hoist to the locomotives that carried everyone through the tunnel. I ran a concrete pump on the graveyard shift midnight to 8 A.M.

I wasn't used to being up all night. After my first shift on my first night, we were riding the train out and I was nodding off. All of a sudden, there was this accident. I opened my eyes and the car was perpendicular to the tracks. We had derailed. I was shitting my pants.

Now we had to walk out, probably a mile, maybe longer. The lighting wasn't good. The air sucked. There was water on the bottom of the tunnel and I'm thinking, "What did I get myself in to?"

But I loved the people I worked with. The sandhogs were just incredible people to work with night after night in such dangerous conditions. It really made me appreciate what I have, to see what some other people have to do to make a living.

I worked down there over a year, and then I had an opportunity to run a backhoe on the ground for a contractor on 1st Avenue, digging sewer lines or something. That was huge for me. I could work normal hours.

At that point, I said to myself, "This isn't a bad living. If I'm going to do it, I want to run a crane. That is what I want to do." That was my dad's claim to fame. He had a stellar reputation.

All on my own, I'd go into Manhattan to job sites with cranes. I'd stand on the running board of the machine and ask the operator a gazillion questions. Once in a blue moon, at lunch time, the operator would say, "All right, kid, go ahead and play with the crane."

The tower cranes, the climbing cranes in the air used on highrises, was the pinnacle for me. When you can run one of those, you've arrived. Operators working in the air have a lot more responsibility. You can't make mistakes, especially in Manhattan. Most side streets are eighteen feet wide, at best. If you're sending even an empty hook down from the fortieth floor, you can't afford to have it drift. You need to be in control all the time. You have to know how to calculate lifting capacity, because the capacity is always changing, depending on the configuration of the crane and how high you are. You have to know the weight of the piece you're lifting. The farther you have to drop a hook down, the less capacity you have. You have to compensate for the weight of the cable and the boom angle.

On that very first job in Manhattan, I had a really bad accident. I was swinging the crane around and the counterweight of the crane, the back end, hit an exterior column that was already in place. When I hit it, the column teetered back and forth. Then the plates let go and it went off the side of the building.

I watched that column fall twenty stories. I had no idea if there were people below. I sat up there for ten or fifteen minutes not knowing what happened.

As it turned out, it fell perfectly horizontal all the way to the street. There were wooden sidewalk bridges covering the sidewalk to protect pedestrians from small pieces of falling debris, but not a whole column. That column took down the bridges on each side of the street and landed between four parked cars. Nobody was on the sidewalk and there was no damage to the cars. All we had to do was repair the sidewalk bridges.

It was a miracle. As soon as we pulled the column out of the street I climbed down the crane and went to a church around the corner. I must have stayed in there two or three hours.

The ironworkers were great. They were worried about *me*.

My license was suspended two weeks while the New York City Department of Buildings did an investigation. Then I was reinstated. I went back to the same site, stayed with that company, and went on to the next job with them.

I've been on cranes ever since, almost twenty-five years now. It's an exciting job. The pay is right. In between jobs you have time off. At 3 P.M. or 4 P.M., you shut the crane off and you're done for the day.

It's a good life.

•   •   •

Although Bovis wouldn't officially take over management responsibility for the site until January, they already were assuming many of those duties by mid-October. Lou Mendes of the DDC ordered representatives of the major contractors to attend the meetings in the Bovis trailer. And Charlie Vitchers, Bovis's daytime supervisor, began to assume a larger role.

CHARLIE VITCHERS

In early October, Jim Abadie basically said to me, "We're going to be running this job, we're going to handle the slurry wall, we're going to be in charge of all of the equipment, we're going to be in charge for accounting for all of the manpower." He knew what was coming down the pike, stuff I didn't know about, from the DDC. Jim explained to me who was staying and who was going, who the supers were going to be, who the laborers were going to be, what contractors belonged to us. We worked on an organizational chart and when we had the organizational chart together, it became apparent who had to be in these meetings.

So I got my shit together pretty quick.

On October 11, my birthday, he told me, "Charlie, gear up. You're going to be the guy. I want you to go to all the meetings. I want you to start taking a more serious approach as to running the meetings."

He basically said, "Charlie, here's the baton."

I'll never forget the first meeting a few days later where I kind of took over. Guys were still coming to the table with plans that showed quadrant demarcation lines. Even though the tieback operation had started on October 12, people were still talking in quadrants. I was getting frustrated. It didn't work and it was never going to work. A dozen guys or more would stand around a table with a blueprint in the middle and you couldn't even see the plan. All everybody did was argue. "What's this guy doing, what's that guy doing?" you know?

Lou Mendes would say, "I want the crane here. Now do it, don't even stay here for the meeting, just go out and do it." There was no communication. We weren't efficient. It made recovery slow, and it just wasn't acceptable to be slow on that job.

So one night later that month I stayed late. I went in the trailer about midnight and I took a big plan of the site and I made an outline of the site and all the buildings on the white board. When I was done I put the outline of the slurry walls, Building Five, Building Four, Building Six, and Building Seven in tape because they weren't going anywhere.

I used dry erase marker for everything else. I drew the donut hole in Building Six. I put every crane on the map, Tully Road, all that kind of stuff. I wanted to be able to track the movement on the field, and using a dry eraser meant I didn't have to keep remaking drawings. I stayed there that whole night making sure it was right. Then I put it up on the back wall of the trailer so that was the first thing anyone saw when they walked in.

At the morning meeting the guys came in and looked at this board. The plan had no demarcations, no quadrants—I never had a quadrant on my drawings. I looked at everybody and said, "It's one site, guys. It's one site. We're never going to be able to handle this job in any other way. There's no such thing as a delineation line between Tully and Bovis or AMEC and Turner and Tully and Bovis. It doesn't work that way. No lines on the plan. We work off of *one plan.*"

Now we weren't fighting over turf. Contractors still worked their quad, but there was coordination.

The outline of every building was there in scale, the positioning of all of the cranes was located on the drawings. I would draw an arc around the crane based on scale and say, "This is the no-fly zone," where we couldn't work because the crane was operating there, then I'd put that on the board. Now guys could go back out into the field and tell their men, "Don't go over there today—they're working on that today."

I numbered the slurry wall panels so now even the cops knew what I was talking about when I referred to an individual panel. They started to understand how to read a blueprint.

Now the job wasn't so confusing. Now we're moving forward.

Before then, people would be in positions where they would hamper somebody else. For instance, when we were using the man basket to pick steel out of the South Tower, it was being handled from a crane with a 350-foot boom on Liberty Street. Con Edison and the Bureau of Water and Sewer Operations needed to get at the watermain that ran up Liberty Street and the gasmain and shut them off. But the matting for the crane was in the wrong spot. The utility guys showed up and started screaming, "The crane's in the way!"

If they had told me two days ago, I would have known. But now everybody could look at the white board and *BING!*—the light goes on. The crane is on the board. And now this guy's thinking, "Oh shit, I got a truck coming here tomorrow, I need access to that area." So now he gets on the schedule. And now Bobby Gray knows we've got to move the crane and Tully knows we have to move the matting. We'll do it between 11 P.M. and 1 A.M. and have the crane repositioned by 7 A.M. in the morning. We had coordination between people who weren't coordinating before.

I'd come in the office sometimes and see guys just staring at the board.

Putting that white board up was very important.

BOBBY GRAY

That was the emergence of Charlie. He filled the void. He said, "Okay, wait a minute, I understand what you want to do but we can't do it that way. We need to stop a second, lace up our boots, and we'll go in and do it this way."

In the trailer and on the pile we could do stuff without going into the bureaucracy. Sammy could go to almost any operator on that site and say, "Could you help me over here?" And Charlie would check it out on his board, go "Uh-huh," and that guy would go down there and help him.

MICHAEL BANKER, FDNY

Once we knew where the contractors were working and everything was marked out, there were maps drawn to give our guys. We could bring information back to the fire department and say, "They're digging over here on Liberty and West, they're going down by the hotel so we need to get crews of spotters over there to watch when they're taking the debris out." Once we got that information, and information from the engineering staff, we were able to find specific columns, then we could see where staircases were located in relationship to those columns, and we found a lot of people. The staircases were always a good source of recoveries.

FATHER BRIAN JORDAN

That trailer was the command center, the inner sanctum, no question. Charlie was undoubtedly one of the greatest leaders at Ground Zero. Why? Because he was smart, experienced, tough, and completely compassionate. He was a great listener, but he could argue with the best of them as well.

I'll sing the same praises of Bobby Gray. He's got an engaging smile and presence, but he'll go right at you—he doesn't suffer fools gladly. At the same time, he's full of compassion. He was one of the first to tell me, "Our guys aren't used to this," to ask "How are we going to deal with this?" Bobby saw everything not only from a macro view, but also from a micro view. He knew what had to be done over the whole sixteen acres, but was always willing to look for advice from others. He engaged their professional expertise, whether they were architects, engineers, EMS workers, ironworkers, or priests. He was an absolute genius at distilling the wisdom of others.

CHARLIE VITCHERS

It just took the DDC to say, "Bovis wants the job. Bovis is running the job." That's all they had to say. It didn't come from us, it didn't come from anybody else. It came from them, and that was it. They needed one of the four main quadrant companies to get it together and they got it.

I was at the white board every meeting and I had everybody's undivided attention. Everybody sat there and watched—this is where we're going to be working tomorrow, this is where we're not going to be working tomorrow, and I'd give them the reasons why. Every day something changed on the job site, but nobody said "boo" until I was done explaining what I thought was going on, and what I thought we were going to move into in the next shift.

I knew every guy in that room on a first-name basis. I would go around the room and ask, "What do you think?" Someone would say, "Charlie, I'm fine with this, but what about this?" So we'd have another five-minute conversation.

I'd go to someone else, "Everything all right out there?" Most of the time it was, or someone would say, "Yeah, Charlie, no problem, everything's cool. But I don't want that grappler operator on the night shift anymore."

"Fine," I'd say, "he's gone." And the guy would be gone that night, no questions asked. Whatever I had to do to keep harmony in the trailer is what I made happen. Nobody walked out of there feeling they were shortchanged.

And no matter what we needed, what we wanted, everybody said, "Yes, yes, yes." Nobody ever said, "No, we can't do it." It was amazing. Basically, after late October, Lou Mendes didn't even bother coming to the trailer meetings anymore. He'd only come when he absolutely had to.

Did I know where every hole was being drilled in the slurry wall? Yes, I did. Did I know how many holes were going to be done by the morning? Yes, I did. Did I know how many tiebacks had been tensioned in the last forty-eight hours, and what the next week was going to look like? Yes, I did. Danny Mirt and I spent hours at the board brainstorming and planning. Because if I could see it on the board, I'd remember it. Then I could sit at a meeting without looking at a drawing and explain where we were. It blew a lot of people away because they were focused on just one thing. But I was focused on everything—where the recoveries were, where the cops wanted to go, where the firemen wanted to go.

It was late October before I finally realized what I had been assigned to do. There were no other general supers coming in.

I'm not a commissioner. I'm not a fireman. I'm not a chief. I'm not a head of construction. I'm just a guy working the field, but certain people seemed to realize that I knew a lot more about this site than a lot of higher-up people. Maybe some of them thought I was the biggest asshole in the world, but what I got from most of the people down there was their respect, because they got mine. If I said something that they didn't like, nobody held back. Some mornings someone would come in like a bull in a china shop. "What happened with this? What happened with that?"

I'd say, "Listen, not everybody is in the meeting yet. We'll start the meeting when everybody's here, okay? Don't come in here and start screaming that you want first priority, you're not the first priority."

Everybody in that room knew we were going to do what we had to do, no matter who yelled and screamed. The agencies, the firemen, the cops, they would have been dead in the water had it not been for somebody keeping harmony between them and the construction industry. I got very friendly with some of the firemen, guys like Sammy and Steve and Mike, because they were doing things the way they should be done and we were having discussions about how everything impacted recovery.

One reason why Charlie Vitchers was able to command the attention and respect of such disparate groups as FDNY and PAPD and tradesmen and contractors, was that he gave the emotional needs on the site the same weight as he gave the logistical demands. He made certain everyone knew that he considered recovery their most important task. But he also was keenly aware of what impact the process of recovery had on everyone.

CHARLIE VITCHERS

Some days Sammy, Steve, or Mike Banker would come in and just sit at the table and have their heads down, and I'd ask, "You guys all right?" They wouldn't say anything. You'd know they just found two of their guys last night, the guy that Mike Banker worked with for three years, and the guy Steve Rasweiler knew for twenty years. They'd spent the whole night digging their buddies out and going to visit their family, but they made it back for the meeting in the morning.

People's emotions changed every day based on what affected them down there. You couldn't take anything for granted, things changed every day. John Ryan of PAPD would come in with tears in his eyes–they just found *his* buddy. You knew John was consoling some guy's widow last night, but he still came back to the meeting the next day. As much as we had our little nit-picking differences, at the end of the day the guys were attached to the site emotionally. I didn't realize how much until I started thinking about it after I left the site. There were many days when the firemen and cops were attending funerals and memorial services during the day and then coming back to the site at night. My own superintendents were having problems because they weren't at home. The outside world had no clue what the guys in the pit and in the trailer were dealing with, what we were collectively doing every day.

I started every meeting by asking how many recoveries there had been on the previous shift. I never stopped asking that question. Recovery was the most important thing. It was always there, it was never going to go away until the last truck was off that site.

CHAPTER SEVEN

RECOVERY

As Charlie Vitchers said, "It was all about recovery."

From the first day to the last, virtually every minute of every hour during nine long months, the recovery of human remains dominated every activity, task, and decision made at Ground Zero.

The challenge facing the workers was not physical but emotional. On the pile they spoke in euphemism—victims became recoveries; finding them, recovery. The specter of death was ever-present.

After the initial weeks, most spotters generally worked on the pile for several weeks at a time before rotating out. Most of the construction workers at Ground Zero, however, worked twelve-hour days for months on end.

CHARLIE VITCHERS

The cops and firemen are trained: they have to deal with dead bodies on their job. But this wasn't a classroom, this wasn't Forensics 101. This was reality. We weren't looking at whole bodies—we were looking at pieces. I saw many firemen just sit down and cry their eyes out for hours. So did a lot of construction workers. So did I.

It was something we had no control over. You just had to deal with it, you had to. You say to yourself, "This is why I'm here—these people have to get out." For us on the pile, the urgency to do the cleanup never took precedence over what we were doing, apart from the fact that in the back of your mind you worried about decomposition. We all knew that the longer those people were out there, the less likely they were to be found and the less likely they were to be identified. We knew DNA degraded over time, and if forensic DNA wasn't found, someone might never be identified. That was the only sense of urgency we had to move the job along as quickly as we could. It wasn't because we wanted the steel out of there so we could rebuild the site.

In the initial days, we reported recoveries to anybody wearing a uniform, a Port Authority cop, a fireman, the FBI, whoever was around. I remember finding plane parts once. Word of mouth on the pile was, "Don't touch them, call the FBI." But when you found body parts, you just called whoever you saw in a uniform. You made a visual report. "Here's a helmet; I think we got something over here." We'd bring the uniformed guy over. He'd identify it as a body, and then it was in the hands of uniformed services. They'd take it out.

Locating and removing human remains at Ground Zero didn't require extensive training. All that was required was that you be there, boots on the ground, with a willingness to look. It was an extraordinarily intimate process. Intact bodies and body parts were found because they were seen or smelled or touched. Physical senses became acute to the task. While firefighters and police officers officially were charged with the recovery of victims, all those on the pile participated. It was impossible not to, for human remains were scattered everywhere.

The firefighters who died in the collapse of the Towers were, in a sense, easier to identify than most of the other victims, for the vast majority wore heavy bunker coats and pants. Made of fire-resistant high-tech materials such as Kevlar, Neoprene, Nomex, and Dermoflex, their clothing was almost indestructible and their fluorescent yellow green trim was comparatively easy to spot amid the debris. Sometimes it was possible to read the name of the firefighter emblazoned on the coat, leading to a quick identification of the victim. When the bodies of firemen were placed in body bags and carried from the pile to the morgue, the firefighters often knew whom, among the lost, they had just found.

Debris in the surrounding area would then be searched closely to ensure that nothing—or no one—was missed. While construction workers helped remove the larger debris, recovery workers used small brushes to clear away dust. Suspect bits of debris would be picked up by hand and examined closely, even smelled. Hand and garden tools would be used to extract the delicate human tissue.

Police officers, while not equipped with heavy bunker coats, were often found in proximity to their guns and gun belts, which also often remained intact. The civilians who died on September 11, however, were much more difficult to find. Their clothing provided little protection. Many had burned in the tremendous fires that raged on those floors above the point of impact. The violence generated by the collapse itself caused indescribable damage. Very, very few civilian bodies were found intact.

Nearly everyone on the pile found themselves instinctively scanning the debris for anything that might be human. It was not uncommon to see a worker walking across the pile stop, pick up some scrap, hold it close to his face, and then, satisfied it was not human, discard it and move on, as if it were the most natural thing in the world.

No one had to tell the searchers about the importance of DNA. Everyone had watched enough television and read enough newspaper stories to know that even the smallest piece of human tissue contained forensic evidence that could lead to the identification of a victim, which would give some measure of peace to a mourning family. The smallest fragments were bagged and delivered to the morgue for identification. The search for remains had its own informal routine, one that evolved on the pile. The official spotters were members of FDNY or PAPD. They both searched the pile on their own, as well as focused their efforts near working grapplers. As the grapplers removed material and the pile was slowly exposed in a given area, spotters would search for remains. The grappler operators then staged debris in a separate pile and spread it out. Spotters searched it once again using garden rakes, hoes, and other hand tools. Once cleared, spotters looked at the material again as it was loaded onto trucks for transfer off-site. The material then went either by truck or barge to the Fresh Kills Landfill in Staten Island. At Fresh Kills, debris was placed on conveyor belts and searched by hand one final time under the direction of FDNY.

CHARLIE VITCHERS

The remains we found were mostly bone fragments. Some of the stuff you found by the smell.

Early on there was no set recovery procedure in place. During the bucket brigades, when anything less than a mostly complete body was found, it was just put in a bucket, then transferred into a red medical waste bag, and transported out on the back of an all-terrain vehicle with a little dump cart on the back, what we called a gator. It went to one of the triage centers, or to the makeshift morgue up on Liberty Street, then later to the Office of the Chief Medical Examiner compound on Church Street.

There were many situations when a piece of steel had to be removed or a section of the body would have to be removed so you could retrieve the other half. I mean it might sound strange, but initially it was just that chaotic. The first couple days, people were just tagging bags. There was no general assignment. Every little group on the pile had red hazardous material bags. Later, it became the responsibility of the fire department or police department to try to get a medical examiner, but as time went on the medical examiners came down to the pile only very rarely. They weren't needed to identify remains in the pile. Usually they were only brought in when a large number of recoveries were found together, to identify the number of bodies so they could be removed separately.

The initial response of everyone who went down there—the firemen, the cops, all the volunteers—was emotional. The bucket brigades were fine, but it was an emotional response. They weren't practical and they didn't retrieve much forensic evidence. We lost a couple of weeks up front just catering to everyone's emotional response on that pile, rather than doing the logical thing, which would have been to pull everybody out and start dismantling the pile systematically, using spotters to look for remains, which is the way it finally evolved.

Again and again, FDNY and PAPD personnel asked construction workers to spread out every bit of material so that it could be gone over, one more time. Just in case. Everyone understood, but the process consumed a great deal of time.

CHARLIE VITCHERS

There were firemen on the pile who had been sleeping next to a guy in the firehouse the night before and all of a sudden he's gone. He's in that pile and the firemen out there knew that there were 300 more out there. The result was a bunch of stressed out people on that pile doing anything and everything that they could think of, which is not necessarily the same as doing anything and everything that they should be doing. From the start, we all should have backed off and established some protocol.

The reason why I won't talk about the details of what we found is very simple: respect for the dead and for the families. When I read graphic descriptions about body parts and bodies, it makes me sad because I think it opens up wounds. Families start wondering if that was someone they lost. They don't need that, it's that simple.

FATHER BRIAN JORDAN

Eighty percent of the recovery workers were from the building and construction trades. They weren't accustomed to seeing all these dead bodies and body parts. EMS, policemen, firemen—they're trained, they have some experience, to a lesser degree of course, to this kind of horror.

The construction guys did not have that training. A lot of these guys were encountering hands and arms and legs and fingers, and just going, "Oh my God." I was trying to be a bridge to help them deal with their feelings because the entire effort depended on them.

Those of us who worked on the pile don't have a high degree of respect for people who are trying to exploit their 9/11 experience. That's why some recovery workers won't talk about what they saw. They're repulsed by people who exaggerate the experience or don't treat it with respect or reverence.

They're still trying to make sense of the experience in their own lives. So am I.

BOBBY GRAY

I am not very comfortable talking about recoveries—that's how we all referred to them, firemen, everybody. It's not that I'm uncomfortable about recoveries themselves, it's just that I have a lot of respect for the victims' families. I'm very reluctant to talk about some of the things that I saw, or heard that others saw, because for the people who never got anything back—no remains whatsoever, about a thousand of them—I can't put them through that.

What the other operating engineers went through regularly . . . I'm sure they try and not dream about it, try to compartmentalize it. Most of us don't talk about it. I certainly don't. And I didn't see as much as most operators did. They were up close and personal to it. Some of them could tell where the recoveries were before the cops or the firemen could—from the smell. They would say, "Hey, you're looking in the wrong place, look over here."

These were all tough people. But it would come up in conversations. Every one of them saw stuff that God never intended people to see. Myself included.

At the beginning there were hundreds of refrigerated box trailers lined up along West Street, no tractors, just the trailers. I remember seeing one open trailer, forty feet long, packed full of body bags. They were there for only one reason. Whoever brought them in thought they were all gonna be filled up.

They weren't.

Once we realized we weren't going to find anybody alive, the next best thing that could happen was to make recoveries. We always held out hope, right down to the last bucket of material that was shaken out and raked, that we might find something with DNA that they could identify someone with. We realized how important one shovelful of material could be.

PIA HOFMANN, OPERATING ENGINEER

I did the best I could as far as looking out and loading up stuff. But some of this stuff you couldn't even see. You always smelled it first.

I don't know how some of these firefighters were able to spot the bodies. Once, I took out a whole grappler claw full of material and put it to the side. The firefighters went over to look and there was a body. I didn't even see it. But then I saw the rest of it in the other pile that I had put to the right of me.

It was very hard. I could smell it before I saw it because everything looked the same.

A native of Germany, Pia Hofmann came to New York at age sixteen to work as an au pair. She stayed, went to school, studied mechanical drafting, and went to work.

"Can you imagine that," she says, laughing. "I actually used to work in an office."

In 1995, after a marriage and divorce, she became a corrections officer at New York's notorious Riker's Island. "I only worked at Riker's Island for a year and a half," she recalls, "a year and a half too long."

At the same time, she went back to school to become a heavy equipment operator. She laughs about that, as well.

"I'd show my friends my crane license and say, 'Do you know what this is? It's my Get-out-of-Jail-Free card.' "

Over time, through a combination of training and on the job experience, Hofmann became a licensed operating engineer. Operating engineers must qualify to run a wide variety of machinery, ranging from small air compressors to bobcats, excavators, backhoes, bulldozers, and cranes. Few are given the opportunity to run the big cranes, which is a pre-

requisite to becoming Master Mechanic, the foreman responsible for all heavy equipment on a job site.

Just prior to September 11, Hofmann earned her class-B license, making her qualified to operate virtually any machine, including big cranes.

PIA HOFMANN, OPERATING ENGINEER

After my divorce, I was really struggling financially. I had looked into becoming a laborer and one day the husband of a friend of mine, a crane operator, helped me out.

He goes, "You know, I'm gonna make you an operating engineer, we're gonna go up to the school and I'm gonna put you on a cherry picker."

I thought he meant one of those small things you see working on the power lines. But they put me right in a big 35-ton crane with rubber tires. I guess they wanted to see right away whether I had a knack for it.

I didn't think I did spectacularly well, but it's not brain surgery. On the way home I asked, "How did I do?"

He goes, "You did great."

Because of that, I got into the union program. Field school was on Saturday and during the week we had classroom work at the union hall.

The classroom work—simple common sense stuff, simple math—wasn't quite quick enough for me. You can get an education, but common sense is something you are born with. I was fortunate; I was born with common sense. And I would say 80 to 85 percent of being an operator is common sense.

As a woman in the profession, you always come across jerks that think you can't do the job. I was on one job and this foreman, a real wise guy, comes up and says, "Oh, what are you here for? To cover the compressor?"

That's an insult because running a compressor is just a baby-sitting job. You don't have to know how to do anything. I said to him, "For your information I'm a crane operator, okay? A *long boom operator.* I am *not here* to cover the compressor."

As much as I think I'm going to get used to that attitude, I'm never going to. I have to prove myself over and over again, on every job.

The first thing I did after the Towers fell was donate blood. It made me feel a little better, until I got home and sat in front of the TV for hours on end, doing nothing but crying. I felt helpless. I finally went to the Union Hall and told the business agent, "Put me on the volunteer list. I need to go down there. All I'm doing is sitting in front of the TV crying."

He goes, "Well, how's your stomach?"

I know he didn't want to send me down there. He didn't want to subject me to that stuff. I think I made him very proud.

Weeks, even months after the attacks, everyone—the operating engineers, spotters, ironworkers—still held on to the dim hope that, somewhere, somehow, they would find survivors trapped deep within the debris. That slim chance drove the workers and kept them at their task day after day, past the point of exhaustion. They knew the clock was ticking.

CHARLIE VITCHERS

The normal cut-off point for a survivor was, I think, twenty-eight days. I believe that's what the fire department went with. But I'll tell you what, sixty days, one hundred days after 9/11, we were all hoping that someone might have found a way to survive down there. Because we didn't know what was below the pile. That's why the firemen and the cops and all the agencies were concerned at how the debris field was going to be picked apart. Nobody wanted to go into that pile and just start ripping steel and tearing stuff out. Nobody. Everybody wanted to get out into that pile and look in every void, and check. Because, God forbid, if we just started ripping shit out, we would desecrate the bodies. You didn't want to find a whole body and then rip it in half just because you didn't give a shit, and you didn't want to impale a section down below, where there might be somebody alive, and kill them. So what do you do?

There were rumors on the site all the time. People would think they'd hear somebody, so we'd tell guys to shut their equipment down. This happened for weeks.

"Did you hear that?"

"What?"

"I don't know, I thought I heard something."

So you'd turn all the machines off and shut down the whole site until it was so quiet you could hear the wind blowing, just because one guy thought he heard something.

You'd ask, "Well, what was it?"

And the guy would just be overwhelmed. He's like, "I don't know, I just thought I heard somebody calling out."

So you'd look. And then you'd start the machinery up and keep going. That happened all the time in the early days. It was pretty intense.

I don't think anybody wanted to believe what we were doing or what we were seeing. From the start, there were reports of body parts and bodies throughout the site. In the beginning the firefighters and the policemen were looking for their own. They had some idea where they might be and figured if they found their own guys, they'd find civilians with them, which was pretty much true.

The firemen did most of the actual extractions of the bodies, and the searches for them, but this wasn't like a typical tenant house fire where the building collapses and after the fire is out you can pick through wood and throw stuff over your shoulder and find what you need and then get out of there and let the demolition crew come in.

I think it took them a while to step back and realize we weren't just going to go out there and find everybody. There was a million tons of steel stuck together and the only way to get it apart and find anyone was for us to burn it, pick it, and move it. We had ironworkers out there burning steel for days and days and days just to get the firemen ten more feet down into the pile so they could jump in the hole with their scrapers and their hand hoes and their pickaxes. When they didn't find anything they'd step back and say, "Okay, continue digging."

As we started to do deconstruction of the site, recovery became a lot more organized because specific people from the fire department were assigned to work with the machinery in an area. People got familiar with one another. Operators worked with a regular team of guys.

As the operator dug, small teams of firemen stood nearby, looking in the pit and looking at what the operator took out. When an operator saw something that resembled a human remain he would alert whoever was working with him. He'd say, "Hey, I think I got a hit over here. This looks like a . . ."–whatever. He'd describe what he'd seen and the fire department would jump down into the debris pile and check it out. If it was a body part, they would stop the operator from digging. Then a couple operators would get together and decide the best way to approach pulling debris out of there. Can we go straight down? Or do we have to dig a twenty-five-foot radius and remove some of the debris that might fall in if we go too deep too fast? That effort came mostly from the operators themselves.

We tried to track where bodies were found on the site. We'd tell the Office of the Medical Examiner, "We found a recovery near the North Bridge," but that didn't mean much to them; it wasn't specific enough. Once we got a little more control on the site and had the equipment, we pinpointed recoveries with GPS equipment. They started using a grid system to track where recoveries were found, which helped them find more. The fire department could look on a map and see visually where clusters of people were being found.

MICHAEL GRAY, OPERATING ENGINEER

The one thing I do remember—and I have never experienced anything like it—was a certain smell that came from an area with bodies in it. I remember one Sunday in particular because on Saturday we hadn't recovered anyone. The firemen hit the remnants of a stairwell probably fifty feet away from my crane and I remember thinking, "This is a good thing."

The firemen asked me to stop the crane because they were concerned about the crane's vibrations causing the pile to collapse. So I stopped and kind of wandered over. I don't know why. Seeing what I saw, I don't think I would do it again. There were nine or ten bodies. I think five of them were firefighters. As long as I live I will never forget the smell. I've never smelled anything like it. You couldn't help but imagine that person's last moments.

Driving home that night I had a cigarette trying to get rid of the smell. But it didn't help. I walked in the house and sat on the bathtub in the bathroom. I was mentally, physically, and psychologically exhausted. My wife came in and asked, "What is that smell?"

"It's death," I said. That's all.

Working recovery on the pile was bigger than any one person. It was something that needed to be done. I didn't lose anybody very close down there, but the idea of trying to bring something back for people became a driving force. To be part of something that was so much bigger than yourself.

BOBBY GRAY

I can't forget the smell. It was so powerful. Three World Financial—the American Express Building—was a temporary morgue in the early days. It was a place we used to walk through as a short cut. I've never forgotten the smell. I can walk into the building today and it comes right back. It's the strangest thing.

I think it's just a memory. I mean, I know it's just a memory. But it was so prevalent, the smell. For so long, it was just so strong.

During the collapse of the Towers, multiple simultaneous processes turned the Twin Towers and their contents into indistinct rubble. Each collapsing floor crushed everything on the floor below. As more floors collapsed downward, the velocity increased, creating an incredible amount of pressure and heat. Everything—steel, concrete, glass, office furniture, elevator cable—was moving and grinding against everything else, generating enormous amounts of friction. The end result was that nearly everything was first crushed flat, then ground together, and finally crushed again when the

Towers hit the ground. Very few items at all, and virtually nothing of any significant size, weight, or bulk, survived the collapse intact.

CHARLIE VITCHERS

Apart from recoveries, we didn't find one thing. Nothing. Not even a file cabinet. When we got into Building Six, which had a big hole in the middle—what we called a donut hole, like you'd cut a section of the building out and exposed different floors like in Oklahoma City—the perimeter of that hole contained furniture and desks and stuff. But it was only a small area, one little section, that was it. In other places there were no desks or chairs or tables or glass or nothing.

As we were working on the pile, people were saying, "We're not finding *anything*."

I'm like, "What do you expect to find?" I mean, almost everything burned. We weren't going to find anything that was made out of wood. But you think we would have found a computer . . .

What was weird is that we did find paper. We found fold-out picture albums of kids, like what you'd put on a desk. We found cell phones. We found shoes. But with regard to furniture, nothing, not a thing, not a desk, not a wall panel. The only interior finishes we found were in the lobby level of Tower Two. The marble floor was still intact. The rugs were there. Some things compressed at the bottom of the pile managed to survive. Little pieces of carpet, stuff like that. In the Vista Hotel we found some stuff in the cellar that hadn't been crushed—kitchenware, knives and forks, bottles of wine. But for the most part there was nothing in the pile of debris that was recognizable. A refrigerator, I mean you'd think you could find a refrigerator, but . . . nothing.

BOBBY GRAY

I don't remember seeing carpeting or furniture. You'd think a metal file cabinet would make it, but I don't remember seeing any, or phones, computers, none of that stuff. There were areas where there were no fires, which is not to say that they didn't experience tremendous heat anyway. But even in areas that never burned we didn't find anything. It was just so hard to comprehend that everything could have been pulverized to that extent. How do you pulverize carpet or filing cabinets?

There was steel cable, though, all over the place. Miles and miles and miles of elevator cables. Sometimes we'd yank on one at Liberty Street and see something move on West Street a hundred yards away.

A couple of times I could actually see floors, literally ten stories, compressed into an area four or five feet high. To see two beams, a few feet apart, knowing that there were ten or twelve floors compressed in between, was mind-boggling.

The stress of working day after day in such an environment put nearly everyone on edge. Add simple physical fatigue, and conflict became inevitable. Small slights and otherwise innocuous events sometimes sparked explosive reactions. Men and women who appeared fine one day would break down the next. Most of those working on the pile knew intellectually that everyone was working under tremendous stress. And they were not completely without resources. Service agencies like the Salvation Army and Red Cross were on-site. But construction workers rarely ask for outside help. They were on the clock, working twelve-hour shifts, and they were determined to see the job through. Many wouldn't stop, even when they should have.

CHARLIE VITCHERS

The emotions got to everybody. Sometimes a grappler operator wasn't digging as carefully as a spotter thought he should, so the guy would make a comment. The grappler operator wouldn't hear him. The spotter would think he was blowing him off. So he'd pick up a piece of steel or a piece of concrete and toss it at the operator. Now you got a confrontation. That happened quite a bit, particularly when a new group of firemen were rotated in and hadn't worked around the machines before.

At one time or another all the agencies threw rocks at the grapplers. All of the agencies yelled at the grapplers; they literally broke windows in the grapplers. I had grappler operators who jumped off machines and had to be held back from getting into fisticuffs with cops and firemen. It was just that the emotions on the site really freaked people out.

I finally had a sit-down meeting with the grappler operators and the cops and the firemen and I let them air it out. I told them, "This isn't a therapy session, this is a put-it-on-the-table session and we'll see what we can work out to solve everybody's problem."

Come to find out the general problem was that spotters weren't paying attention to the grappler operators and the grappler operators didn't want to hurt anybody. I understood their concerns, because if you get caught between the tracks and the body of the machine, it's going to cut you in half like a guillotine. There's just no coming back from accidents like that.

PIA HOFMANN, OPERATING ENGINEER

How any of the spotters didn't get killed down there is beyond me. I came very close one day. You grab it here, you put it there, and you get in a mode, okay? But you don't stop those machines on a dime. I had a grappler full of rebar that I was moving from here to there, to get loaded out. I swung to my left and, jeez, all of a sudden there was a firefighter walking right in my path. If he hadn't ducked, his head would have come off. I don't know how I missed him.

He says, "Oh, I'm sorry, I'm sorry."

"You're sorry?" I say. "I would have been more sorry if I had ripped your head off, which I came very close to."

BOBBY GRAY

One day I met an ironworker on the site who I hadn't seen in years and we're talking. They were doing a recovery right next to us with a priest and they put the remains in the body bag. We took our helmets off as they did a little prayer. Then they took off with the body and we just started talking again like nothing happened.

Both of us caught it at the same time. We said to each other, "This is so fucked up. This is all so horrendous, but it's common now." You almost became numb to it.

CHARLIE VITCHERS

I remember an ironworker out cutting steel on the pile one day. I was handing him hoses. He was just burning away and then all of a sudden he shuts off his torch and he sits down, right in the middle of everything, not moving. I went out there and said, "What's up?"

He points down to his feet.

He'd been standing in what was left of a body, burning steel, without knowing it. When he realized it, he just couldn't handle it. He shut his torch off, he sat down, and he couldn't go on. We had to pull him off the pile. The guy left the site. He never came back.

I could understand that. It was fine, you know? It didn't mean he was a wimp. If you have to leave the site, then leave the site.

FATHER BRIAN JORDAN

I told some guys to go home. I spoke to Ken Holden and his staff at the DDC about the emotional impact this was having with the people working on the pile. I said, "There are certain people you may want to ask to go somewhere else." He agreed. We did that quietly, so we could protect the personal integrity of each person.

I could see the burnout. I could see their horror. I could see guys just shaking, on the verge of a breakdown.

BOBBY GRAY

One operator who came down was a Vietnam vet. He still had problems from that but he wanted badly to be on the site and help.

I'll never forget it. Tully had taken over a Chinese restaurant on Liberty Street. The prevailing winds always seemed to be blowing from that direction. That corner was always smoky and the odor was always very strong.

One day, this operator and I were walking around the site and got to this restaurant. Something about the paintings on the wall and the smell from the pile just hit him all at once. He lost it and started to shake. He was almost in tears. He said to me, "I just can't stay here. The smell . . ."

That was the straw that broke the camel's back for him. I had people working for months who all of a sudden said, "I can't do this anymore." They saw just one thing, whatever it was, and that was it. They'd had enough and had to admit, "Look I need a break," or "I gotta get out." That took a lot of strength.

CHARLIE VITCHERS

A lot of guys came down and lasted only a day or so and then requested to be transferred out. I don't know what happened to some of them after that. For Bovis, Jim Abadie made the final decision about who was going to stay. If an individual decided he couldn't handle it, he either spoke to me or he spoke to Jimmy. We had to decide who was capable of staying.

I know some guys, they're zombies today. They'll never be right

9/23/01: Fires burned at Ground Zero from September 11 until mid-December.

9/26/01: By late September, cranes ringed the site and hundreds of workers pored over the rubble, cutting steel and looking for remains.

10/05/01: Ironworkers worked day and night cutting steel apart with torches so it could be safely removed by operating engineers using cranes and grapplers.

10/07/01: In early October, ironworkers in a man basket used torches to cut down the standing facades of the towers in a procedure they called a "hair-cut."

10/26/01: Construction workers, firemen, and police all pause as five victims are recovered in late October.

11/08/01: Operating engineers running grapplers formed a "daisy-chain," transferring debris off the pile and spreading it out so spotters could search for remains.

2/10/02: Debris was trucked off-site on the "Tully Road," a pathway built on collapsed rubble.

2/10/02: In mid-February workers discovered the remains of two firefighters compressed between floors in the debris beneath Tully Road.

3/30/02: The removal of the last column from the South Tower, engraved "1001B," marked a symbolic end to the cleanup and recovery of Ground Zero.

3/30/02: Fearing that the slurry wall would collapse and flood the site, engineers reinstalled "tiebacks" that anchored the wall to the surrounding bedrock, a process that began in October and lasted until the final days.

5/01/02: By May, only sub-grade remnants of Building Six *(left)* remained in the pit.

5/25/02: Every morning Charlie Vitchers *(right)* met in "the trailer" with construction supervisors, administrators, police, and fire personnel to discuss the days' activities and logistics.

5/20/02: The recovery of human remains was an extraordinarily intimate process. Even as the job was coming to a close, workers pored over the dust and debris.

again. They're still suffering the effects of what they saw on the pile. Personally, I'm glad I wasn't down there standing on West Street when those buildings came down. I don't know if I could have handled that. I know one guy who watched the second plane fly over his building. He told me about watching people jump out windows, very matter-of-fact. You don't forget. Ever.

There were so many emotions down there. A lot of relationships got fucked up. Marriages and divorces, breakups between these guys and their girlfriends. They'd tell me, "She doesn't understand me anymore, what I do down there." I heard a lot of hard luck stories. A lot of people from the construction industry are still suffering psychological effects from what went on down there.

HOLLY VITCHERS

Charlie wasn't around on weekends at all and came in late every night. I hardly saw him that whole time, really.

I remember saying to him once, "*Where do you live?* Do you live *here* or do you live *there?*" The truth of the matter was that they lived *there*, all of them. Even when they were home, they were there.

I know they had counselors down there, but I don't know if the guys ever went to them. You're dealing with a very macho crowd. It's pride, maybe, or just the "I'm a man, I can handle it" kind of attitude.

Charlie held it in for quite a while. I don't know whether it was emotionally easier for him earlier or later. I guess it was more horrible in the beginning. The first reaction when you start finding the remains of people can't be good, it can't be good.

MICHAEL GRAY, OPERATING ENGINEER

People were there for a reason. The vibe was good down there. But when they left the site, life had gone on in other places. That was striking. Being on the pile was a different experience, another world unto itself.

Working down there had life-affecting changes on me, but I don't think I ever sat down with somebody who I didn't think would understand. I'd talk about it and tell stories about it with people who were down there. But as far as sitting down with somebody who hadn't been there? Well, I guess I share a little bit, but nothing personal, nothing about how I felt about it.

FATHER BRIAN JORDAN

I used to tell the construction workers down there, "You have to talk about this." When a police officer left the site, he had to go through a required four hours of counseling. And all the firemen were given that option—which should have been mandatory. But no counseling was given to the construction workers at the time, which was wrong. At my weekly sermons I'd keep telling them "You've got to talk with someone, you can't keep it in. You have to talk about this because you have to be able to come to work tomorrow—we've got to do this. No man, no woman is an island."

CHARLIE VITCHERS

I had victims' families ask permission to come in at night and light candles in front of 90 West Street, which was inside the perimeter. They wanted to stay for as long as they could. We'd sneak them in the back gate and let them light their candles. They'd leave all kinds of stuff. One of the victims was in the middle of reading a book when the attacks happened, so the family members brought the book to the site and left it on a piece of steel in front of 90 West Street. We'd let the stuff pile up until we had to move it out.

Other times you'd run into somebody with flowers in their hands and they'd ask, "Can you bring these into the site for me? Just get them as close to Tower One as you can."

You couldn't say no. So there I'd be, hiding a set of flowers under my jacket and placing them on the site, knowing that fifteen minutes from now they were probably going to get rolled over by something.

But I'll tell you what, sometimes I'd go down there forty-eight hours later and the flowers would still be there.

For days, even weeks after the attacks, crowds would gather around the perimeter, cheering and applauding the construction workers coming off the site. Members of FDNY became instant heroes. Houses all across America sported American flags and bunting that proudly proclaimed, "We will never forget."

America had united behind those who had perished on September 11. And they united behind those who were working to bring them home.

But such impassioned support could not last. As the days shortened and winter approached, the crowds around the perimeter of Ground Zero began to thin.

BOBBY GRAY

I never felt like I was a hero and I still don't. I feel lucky to have been there, but I think a lot of people outside needed a label to put on the people that were down there. "Hero" was one of them. I knew that was going to be short-lived. As phenomenal as it was to walk out of there or drive out and have people applauding you, I also knew that it was not going to last forever. It was going to stop one day and we'd still have to come back to this job, which was hard and sometimes miserable. We weren't going to have that push from the public saying, "Great, keep going, thank you, thank you, thank you, thank you, thank you." In their hearts and their minds, I'm sure it was still there, but the physical part of that was going to be gone.

I think what happened is that, collectively, Ground Zero receded into itself. It was impossible for the energy level we had over the first few weeks to just keep going. Once it became the grim task it became and we weren't getting accolades anymore, that's when I think all of us on the pile just came together. That's when the "outside" world was created and when "our world" was created. And that's how it stayed until the end. I don't think we realized it, but to me, looking back, I think that's what happened.

You were living, breathing, sleeping that job. At one point I even started thinking, "Why do I go up to Bronxville to go to sleep? I should just live here. It would be so much easier." One night I stayed in a nearby hotel and I thought to myself, "This is great. It's right here." I could get up, look out the window, and see the site.

I used to go to an old chapel in the bottom of one of the buildings nearby and just sit there. Sometimes, I'd go down to the marina off South End Avenue, just to get away. There were still boats anchored there, covered in dust. I would walk down there and look over at New Jersey. And I hate New Jersey. But there was a crane working on a building over there. It was "normal."

Then I'd turn around and be right back in the thick of it.

The longer one stayed at Ground Zero, the more normal it became. When the workers left the site and heard Ground Zero being discussed or mentioned, it wasn't any place they recognized. What the public knew of their world from the few news reports that touched on the cleanup had little to do with their reality. Reporters weren't talking to them—they weren't allowed on-site and besides, the DDC had told the workers if they talked with the press, they'd be fired.

The job was so big, the experience so intense, the emotions so raw, that most couldn't discuss it with anyone not working at Ground Zero anyway. Already, most had broken the world into two distinct areas—their work and the "outside." And the outside was a place they didn't know anymore. A place where people watched television and went to work and ate in restaurants and laughed.

As difficult as it was to be at Ground Zero, it was becoming even more difficult to be away. The pile had become home, a place they felt comfortable, a place where they belonged, a place where they were understood. The outside was becoming ever more remote. And it was becoming more and more difficult to move between the two worlds.

BOBBY GRAY

Those of us on the pile were just going through the motions of normalcy, pretending everything was okay. Families suffered. Wives suffered and husbands suffered. The way I treated my girlfriend Jo-Ann . . . she had become an outsider.

The first night I came home, the very first night, was after the first two or three days working on the site. Jo-Ann was at my apartment. I remember walking up there and I was fine. I didn't feel anything until I got three steps onto the patio and that was it. I just lost it. I almost had a breakdown. She was like, "What's the matter, what's the matter?"

I couldn't tell her, because I didn't know, really.

In retrospect, I was horrible to her. All I could think was, "She's not part of this, she doesn't understand it, and she'll never understand it." And I really was horrible to her. I really don't have an excuse, but that was the mind frame I was in: she wasn't there, she wasn't part of it, she's never gonna understand.

Looking back, I'm surprised she would even talk to me at all.

Jo-Ann Farley works in computer consulting. A divorced mother of two daughters, Farley met Gray at Mercy College. They have known each other for nearly thirty years and have been together for nearly a decade.

JO-ANN FARLEY

The times when he was home, it was like he wasn't there. I don't think he was even aware of what was happening in his life outside the pit. It defined him for that time period. I kept after him to back off, but he was obsessed with getting the site cleaned up, obsessed.

When he did come home he was a shambles. I'd see him walking across the deck into the back door and he'd just be covered in that dust and looking down and *so* tired and just *so* forlorn.

He'd collapse and after about three or four hours' sleep, he'd get up and do it again. Nothing could have stopped him. Nothing did stop him. Nothing could.

People don't realize how much these people sacrificed. Or what their families gave up. It was very, very hard. Brutal. The men who worked there missed everything, everything that a family does. For nine months, they were just gone.

One time he said to me, "I haven't even seen you. You haven't been here."

And I said, "Robert, I've been here every three days. Every three days I get someone to cover the kids. I come over to your house and I do your laundry. I put juice and beer in the refrigerator. Where do you think the beer and the juice are coming from? Are they magically appearing? What do you think happens with all your clothes that are covered with dust?"

He didn't even know. He was completely surprised.

He said, "You've been here every three days?"

He had no idea. It was a total surprise. He was like, "Really? Really?"

Of course it's nothing compared to what it was like for the people who actually lost family members in the Trade Center. But the people who worked on the site took it on themselves to sacrifice a year of their lives, and their families sacrificed too.

They were like brothers in arms. They really, really looked out for each other. They grew to love each other, really love each other, and draw strength from one another.

SAM MELISI, FDNY

My wife kept our family together for seven months. She made every decision, she did everything. I wasn't even part of the family anymore. Everybody would say, "Oh, you did such a good job down there," and I'd say, "My *wife* did the good job." All I did was go to work.

It was emotionally tough to be there every day. It was even tougher on the family members. My son was eight and a half, and my daughter was five. That was tough times. When I'd get home they would be asleep because it would be late, and I'd leave early in the morning and they would still be sleeping. I wanted so much to wake them but I didn't dare.

It is hard to describe the urgency to get back to that site to find out what was happening. It was almost like you were afraid you'd miss something, something might have happened, maybe some recoveries, or a good lead on where more people might be found. It was a tough seven months.

CHARLIE VITCHERS

People didn't want to leave. There were people who were being transferred to another job and I'd say good-bye to them. Then at midnight when I was leaving I'd run into them out in the street, and they'd be drunk, throwing rocks and shit and pissed off.

I had a guy threaten me one night. "Why did they throw me out of here? I'm gonna fucking kill you."

He was gonna kill me because he thought I was the reason he got taken off the job site. Then I saw him on a job about a year and a half later. It was like nothing happened. He didn't remember it.

BOBBY GRAY

I've been asked this question a lot: "What made these guys and these women keep coming back day after day or night after night?" I didn't really have an answer then, but in hindsight, you never left there, you know? You drove home and it was on your mind. You sat at the table with your family and you had dinner and it was your prevailing thought. You went to sleep thinking about it. You dreamt about it. You woke up thinking about it. My answer should have been, "It's not a question of what makes them come back. It's that they never leave."

I'd go to bed thinking about it and wake up and say, "Oh God, this is what I gotta do today."

I would wake up and have an agenda of stuff that I knew I needed to get done. That is not me—I'm not a morning person. But it was so all-encompassing, I couldn't wait to get back. It's hard to explain. That's all I did for months and months, work and go home to sleep.

We called everything else the "outside" or the "outside world." That was weird. I remember I came home one night and I was going to go down to the local pub, where I'd gone many times before, and sit with my friends. I came home, showered, got dressed, went down. I opened the door and there were people laughing, people smoking, drinking. I didn't even go in. I closed the door and went home.

It was a hard thing to leave our world. I think the biggest fear we had was leaving all of the people, the support group. That was the thing that scared most of us, even me.

I was like, man, I gotta go back to the real world someday. I gotta go back to the outside world.

CHAPTER EIGHT

DIGGING IN

By November 1, the amount of progress at Ground Zero was obvious even to an outsider. The haircut procedure had brought down the façades of the South Tower to street level. Within the slurry wall, only the twisted shrouds of the North Tower and the remnants of Building Six loomed over the site. In only seven weeks nearly half a million tons of material had been removed.

The visible destruction wrought on September 11 was disappearing. As it did, so did public interest in the site. The crowds of hundreds of people who once cheered the workers as they left the site each day had dwindled to a few dozen. Hundreds of truckloads of steel, cable, and debris were being shipped off-site each day. Where debris removal proceeded below street level, the pile was becoming a pit. Although fires still burned in a few places underground, most had already exhausted the fuel contained within the pile. As workers dug deeper, they began to encounter both intact columns and concrete slabs held together by rebar from the sub-grade structures. They also began to encounter significant amounts of "Tower dust." Material at the bottom of the pit, which had been pulverized most savagely, had burned in the fires for weeks. The ash, when combined with the hundreds of thousands of gallons of water, turned into a fine muck that dried into a grayish white powder. And it was everywhere.

Ground Zero had been tamed. To those who worked there every day, the pile was no longer incomprehensible. Remaining steel columns were not ran-

dom pick-up sticks, but could be identified within a structural context. New tiebacks were being installed in those portions of the slurry wall now exposed. There was no longer any fear that the wall would be breached and the site filled with water. Engineers had mapped conditions within the underground levels inside the bathtub and workers oriented themselves on the site not in terms of what had fallen, but of what remained.

Outside the slurry wall, on the eastern edge of the site, the shells of Buildings Five and Four stood, awaiting demolition. Renovation work was beginning on World Financial Three. Ninety West Street and 130 Liberty Street were turned over to their owners and stood sealed and empty, wrapped in protective black and orange netting, their demolition or reconstruction scheduled for some indefinite time in the future.

A rough organization was in place. There was communication between contractors, tradesmen, the fire department, and police personnel, and a consensus of sorts had been reached with regard to procedure. While Ground Zero would never be as clearly organized as a normal work site, what had evolved in the trailer was working; the site settled in. Alas, it was not to last.

On the first day of November, New York mayor Rudy Giuliani ordered city officials to limit the number of rescue workers trying to recover victims' bodies to twenty-five members each from FDNY, PAPD, and NYPD, plus an additional ten firefighters for fire suppression, a drastic reduction from the usual eighty to one hundred and fifty firefighters working each shift on recovery efforts. Most of those remaining would be confined and called out to do recoveries only after remains were uncovered during cleanup activities, rather than actively searching for recoveries themselves. City officials publicly cited safety concerns as the reason for the change, calling the site "a disaster waiting to happen."

There was some truth to the city's concern over safety, but at play, as well, were concerns about the cost of overtime, the issue of staffing at firehouses elsewhere in the city, and most insidiously, the growing battle over who controlled Ground Zero. Purely by accident, the events of September 11 had empowered the fire department. At Ground Zero, they had made it clear that they would spend as much time as it took to recover their still-missing members, and they didn't give a damn what that cost. That argument resonated with the public. But city officials feared seeing the firemen heralded as heroes day after day in the New York tabloids and on the evening news. Without the fire department slowing them down, some officials believed the cleanup could go much faster. Looking to the future, they feared the impact 9/11 might have on union contracts. FDNY had to be reeled back in.

The firefighters didn't buy the safety excuse. More than 200 firefighters were still missing and untold numbers of civilians. From the thousands of bodies and body parts recovered thus far, medical examiners had positively identified only 465 victims. Thousands of lesser body parts awaited DNA testing, a lengthy process just getting under way, for never before had such testing been done on such a huge scale. Even though the official list of casualties had dwindled almost daily since September 11, as city officials cross-checked lists of those feared lost, more than 4,000 people were still officially considered missing.

The firefighters believed the city's decision to limit the number of men on the site was based purely on economics, an excuse to increase the speed of debris removal and cut back on overtime pay. They resented the fact that the city wanted to give PAPD and NYPD an equal role in the recovery effort. With fewer firefighters actively searching on-site, they believed fewer human remains would be found. But mostly they feared that the mayor's decision was the first step in a plan to transfer virtually the entire recovery operation to Fresh Kills, where the debris was broken down and sorted by size in monstrous hoppers known as grizzlies. While that may have been an understandable approach for material already searched at Ground Zero, recovery workers blanched at the thought of unsearched debris that likely contained sizable remains being carted off-site in dump trucks and treated so crudely, never mind the risk to any forensic evidence.

And so, on the morning of November 2, more than 1,000 off-duty fire-fighters held a rally to protest the decision.

CHARLIE VITCHERS

You could never prove it on paper, but the conversation in some of these DDC meetings was that they wanted the equipment out that was not essential to reconstruction or the completion of the tiebacks. They were trying to make us get rid of the pieces of equipment that were useful for recovery, to just stick to construction activity. I could see it coming. The DDC would tell me, "We've got to get rid of two more grapplers . . . Let's get the long arm crane out of here . . . Let's get this other stuff out, we're not paying for it anymore."

What the DDC wanted was never gonna happen. It went in one ear and out the other with us. We were not getting rid of this equipment. We were gonna continue searching because there was still thousands of tons of debris out there that still needed to be searched for people.

As far as the DDC was concerned, debris did not need to be searched until it got to the landfill in Staten Island. That was the way they felt. They thought the fact that we were raking through material in the pit was bullshit. But the way debris was being searched in Staten Island had a lot of victims' families upset. Everybody had an issue with what was going on over there because they felt that the grizzlies destroyed forensic evidence. The DDC was even thinking of bringing grizzlies to the pit to sift material before just dumping everything in Staten Island.

In late October, they had told me they wanted to cut the number of firemen on the pile in half and get rid of them. I just bit my tongue. Because I knew, and I hate to say it, but the construction workers and recovery workers were in control of what was happening down there in the pit, not the DDC.

I told the firemen what was coming. "Listen," I said, "the DDC is going to try to cut you guys in half and get rid of you."

I'm not stupid. I wasn't going to keep it to myself and let these guys get blindsided.

There was a big ruckus over that. They almost had a riot.

We—meaning the recovery workers, and I considered myself a recovery worker down there before and above anything—played hardball with the DDC. When the firemen showed up on-site that day, our guys were standing on the machines, protesting and saying, "We're not gonna go back to work unless you keep the firemen on the job site."

The cops tried to keep the firemen from coming on to the site that day. The firemen knocked the gate down, a couple of cops got punched out, and a couple of hundred firemen walked on to the job site. They ended up arresting some firemen who were charged with trespassing, disorderly conduct, resisting arrest, that kind of stuff.

So all of a sudden, after a couple of months of doing recoveries down there, now the DDC was telling us we had to operate in a whole totally different manner. They were proposing that after each recovery the firemen were supposed to stay confined in a bullpen. They wanted only one or two spotters with each piece of equipment. Only if there was a recovery could the other guys leave the bullpen and go help.

It was comical because the DDC had explained this to me, not to the fire department. I was told to create these bullpens. So I went down to the pit, grabbed a couple of forklift operators, and had them grab some concrete Jersey barriers and make these little bullpens.

The fire department basically said to the DDC, "Screw you. We're gonna continue doing what we're doing. Our guys are not gonna sit in a bullpen. We're gonna have our guys with the equipment, and where there's no equipment we're going to keep wandering over the site, looking and digging by hand." So the bullpens sat empty. They were there, but they were never used.

The issues raised by the near riot angered many of the families of missing firefighters who demanded to meet with city officials. On November 12, they met with representatives of the Office of Chief Medical Examiner and the DDC to air their concerns over the recovery process. They made it clear that they would resist any attempt to make the recovery of victims less of a priority and any attempt to cut back on recovery efforts at Ground Zero. The angry, contentious gathering ended any notion city officials still held that debris removal would ever hold sway over the recovery effort.

JIM ABADIE, BOVIS

There was a massive amount of pressure behind-the-scenes to finish the job quickly. But we couldn't just go fast—and there was a lot of infighting over that. There were some ugly, ugly meetings I was at. Then the DDC and OCME went to a victims' meeting and they got lambasted. They came back and said, "Listen, let the firemen do this, and it'll be what it will be."

We were all under a lot of pressure. I always felt it was my role to make sure that we had the right equipment on the job and we weren't wasting money, that we did the job as economically as possible and with as much sensitivity as possible. That was important, too.

CHARLIE VITCHERS

Raking through the debris on-site by hand looking for remains made total perfect sense because what you thought was a rag could have been a piece of flesh, but you couldn't tell unless you held it up in front of your face and got a good look at it. We were determined to find everybody and everything we could, but so much wasn't recognizable. Everything was one color, some of it was wet, some of it was dry—don't forget they hosed the site down constantly for dust suppression. The longer we were there and the deeper we got into the pile the debris was almost like topsoil. Everything was covered with gray dust and dirt. But the guys that were trained, the firemen and the cops that were raking, they knew what they were looking for and they would find stuff and just put it off to the side. When the firemen raked, they always had a bucket of stuff that they thought might have been human remains. The guys would see something and they'd put it in a bucket and that bucket went up to the medical examiner's office.

They would throw any clothing they found in 55-gallon barrels with plastic bags in them. My laborers would wrap them up and drive them to the morgue. They filled buckets up with rings and coins and jewelry, all of that stuff they found raking. They found wallets, they found holsters from cops, they found the guns that the cops were wearing. Maybe they never found the cop, but they found his gun. It was a lot easier for families knowing that they were there, that somebody just didn't disappear.

To me, finding evidence was a big part of being down there, to bring some closure to the families. In talking to some of the victims' families I met, they all said the same things, "They found my husband's watch," or "They found his ring."

Everything was under control except the push to finish fast.

• • •

Even before the push to de-emphasize recovery efforts, those who worked at Ground Zero did not trust the motivation of top DDC administrators, who didn't have a daily presence and a respected role on the pile. After the riot, that distrust calcified. As Ground Zero became ever more manageable, site administrators began to reassert their authority over day-to-day operations. Workers felt a growing sense of responsibility to one another and the victims. Their circle was growing smaller and tighter. An "us against them" mentality festered. The workers had taken possession of the job, and in the upcoming months they would fight to retain it. They resented interference of any kind, particularly if they believed that it wasn't justified and hampered the recovery effort.

While the families of the victims didn't have a presence in the pit, they had strong advocates in Charlie Vitchers and the other workers, who never forgot that the reason they were all there was not because two buildings had fallen, but because when they had, thousands had died and needed to be found.

CHARLIE VITCHERS

The DDC guys in the field every day were fine; their egos were not in the pit. It was the guys coming out of the office that really threw a wrench into everything.

Everybody had to be careful what they said to the DDC because if you rubbed them the wrong way you could be gone no matter how important to the job you thought you were. I had to have construction guys who wouldn't break under stress, who could handle it if somebody got up in their face and started yelling, guys who could walk away and shrug it off and discuss it on a level that wasn't gonna produce a major blowup.

One night, one of the DDC boys came up to me and said, "I want this grappler operator fired."

"Why?" I asked.

He says, "Because he told me to go fuck myself."

I said, "Well, you shouldn't be talking to him."

If that DDC guy had any legitimate concerns about anything the operator was doing, he should have spoken to someone like me first. He only wanted the operator to stop working so he could walk around the machine and then down into the pit.

I said, "So you want me to tell him to stop?"

He says, "Yeah."

"No," I said. "You go fuck yourself." And then I walked away. He grabs my tag, looks at my name, and writes it down.

The next morning I get a call from another DDC guy. He tells me, "You really shouldn't have said that to him because he put it down in the report."

I said, "Good, give me a copy so I can hang it on my wall. I don't have time for this bullshit. If the guy had a problem he should have gone through channels: the guy shouldn't have directly approached the grappler operator because now I got a pissed off grappler operator who wants to hit him in the head with his boom the next time he walks by. Keep that guy out of the field; he's got no business in the pit."

I went to bat for people they wanted off the job. But there were times when no matter how much yelling and screaming I did, I'd lose. I lost this guy Kevin because he had his mask off to smoke a cigarette. He even went up to DDC headquarters himself and apologized and said, "Look, I'm sorry that I got a little upset, but this really doesn't warrant my getting fired."

And he still got fired. Then I wrote a letter and got him back and he was given a warning. A week later Michael Burton at the DDC found out and wanted to know why Kevin was still on the site and that was it, he had to go. When it got to that level you really couldn't argue with it.

Burton even threatened to fire me. I could count on two hands the number of times he closed the door with me in the room and said, "I'm gonna fire you if you don't do it my way. You don't listen to what I'm saying, Charlie? You're fired, you get it? Fired. F-I-R-E-D. Now go out there and do what I just told you I wanted done."

It took all the energy in my body to stay. I'd just shake my head and say, "Yeah, Mike, no problem," and walk out. This is the shit they put you through. There was a lot of that. So it was very important to have guys on the job who could deal with the bureaucratic bullshit.

BOBBY GRAY

I was always behind the operators 110 percent. As Master Mechanic, my job was to make sure they worked safe and did what the contractors needed them to do. There was one instance where a guy was trying to load a column on a truck. It was at night and the column was pretty heavy. Steel on steel, the column slipped out of the grappler. This guy had probably loaded eighty trucks the night before. He had been there for a long time, producing night after night after night and knew what he was doing.

Anyway the column slipped out and crushed the flatbed tractor trailer. The column was probably askew and he probably got part of the weight on the trailer and as soon as he did that it just slipped. There was nothing he could do about it; it was something that was bound to happen sooner or later.

When I came in that morning the operating engineer was still there and he says, "I got fired."

I said, "You got fired? For what?" And he explained the whole story to me.

I said, "Come on," and we went up to the trailer to see the contractor. I went in and I asked, "Okay, what happened?"

He says, "Well, he crushed a trailer, we don't want him around anymore, we want him fired." They wanted to fire a guy who had been out there for weeks just doing his job, and doing it well.

I said, "Okay, no problem. If you want to fire him, let's fire him." And I turned around and started to walk out. The operator looked at me like he couldn't believe what I had just said.

Then I turned back to the contractor and said, "By the way, from now on we're gonna have ironworkers weld eyes on every single piece of steel that we load onto a truck. And we're going to attach solid rigging on every single piece of steel just to make sure this never happens again."

It would have taken forever to do that.

I walked out and before I could get two steps, the contractor says, "Could we reconsider this?"

Long story short, he wasn't fired.

CHARLIE VITCHERS

You needed a clear head down there because there were so many entities to deal with. I mean, I didn't even have my first beer until December. I didn't want to drink. I just couldn't.

I was always there, I was always on call. Whenever I left that site,

I usually just went home and stayed home. Holly and I would just stay together. Or I would go out to see my kids, take them to dinner, and have a night with them or something like that. But the job wasn't discussed.

My days were normally sixteen- to eighteen-hour days. Some nights, after showing up at 5:30 in the morning, I'd say to myself, "Listen, I'm going to get out of here by 9 o'clock tonight." And I wouldn't get out of there until 12:30 A.M. I just went home and went to sleep and got up and came back to the site.

I don't think I took my first day off and first trip home to Pennsylvania until early November. It was the first time since September 11 that I actually got in a car alone and left the site.

I went over the George Washington Bridge, came out of the tunnel, then looked behind me and saw this billow of smoke.

I lost it. I cried the whole ride up.

A massive amount of work remained, including one potential hazard that had dogged the engineers from day one.

The Towers had been cooled by a series of massive chillers, located in the mechanical rooms on the lower levels of the substructure. These units held some 200,000 pounds of Freon, a fluorinated hydrocarbon used in refrigeration and air-conditioning. When stored under pressure, Freon is a nonflammable liquid and is relatively safe to use.

But if it is depressurized—which can happen when a jumbo jet, cruising at 500 miles per hour, smashes into a 110-story skyscraper causing a catastrophic collapse of all 110 stories directly on top of the pressurized storage units—Freon will revert into a gaseous form. Though it is not toxic in and of itself, it is heavier than air and in a confined space, gaseous Freon will immediately displace oxygen. Anyone working within that space will suffocate.

In September, engineers had determined that, shortly after the collapse of the Towers, the Freon contained in the main chiller plant had dissipated. What they feared was that the secondary chiller unit, which had been put in after the 1993 bombing, remained intact, buried far beneath the debris near the North Tower.

To site administrators and those on the outside, Freon loomed as a danger almost as serious as the potential failure of the slurry wall. It had been identified as a risk from the start, and as excavation and demolition activities approached the secondary chiller plant, those concerns became more pronounced. Fear of Freon began to spread among the workers, particularly among those who were not familiar with it.

At the same time, however, there were dozens of people for whom Freon was just another of the many potential hazards that existed on virtually every construction site. Those who had actually worked in and around Freon—a common experience for anyone who had either installed HVAC cooling systems or worked in their proximity—understood the risk. More importantly, they understood how to avoid turning the potential hazard into a present danger.

CHARLIE VITCHERS

Freon is used in cooling systems. In the liquid state, like when it's pressurized in a chiller, it's no problem. It's not combustible. But when it hits the air it turns back into vapor. Freon is heavier than air, so it displaces oxygen. Like carbon monoxide, it can be an invisible killer. If you breathe it in, you'll suffocate. There were thousands of gallons of Freon that we were concerned with down there that we thought might be intact.

During the Tower collapse, any Freon in the main chiller plant blew out; the collapse itself probably pushed it out and it was gone. The only Freon that we were still worried about was in what we called the North Projection. I think there were twelve small chillers that helped chill and cool Building Six and parts of Tower One. We knew the chiller plant was compromised and buried under debris. I knew what I was looking at when we excavated the site. I knew the mechanical equipment rooms. I'd hung Sheetrock in them and hung doors in them and changed hardware. I had been a carpenter down there.

There was a guy named Frank, who was the chief engineer who ran the mechanical plant of the World Trade Center. On September 11, he got away with his life. But he came back when we needed to find the chiller plants and the Freon tanks.

We went down there in the North Projection with about 600 feet of hose and put a monitor in the chiller room. It came up with a reading like 0.0025 percent Freon, which is nothing. It wasn't there; it wasn't a problem, and we monitored it the whole way through.

The DDC made a bigger stink out of it than they should have. It slowed a lot of people down and was a needless worry people threw out into the field that could have created a panic. The concern was that operators working in the area wouldn't know if their cab was filling up with Freon, and that created a lot of anxiety among the grappler operators–they didn't want to die.

So the DDC instituted protocols and procedures and spent hundreds of thousands of dollars on Freon monitoring. We put Freon monitors in all of the cabs of the machines and we gave the operators emergency Scott packs, little oxygen tanks. If they ever felt dizzy they could get some fresh oxygen and get the hell out of the cab.

It was all bullshit. Freon isn't a threat unless you're in an enclosed space and it gets loose on you. That wasn't gonna happen. Nobody was really working below grade. It wasn't a confined space anyway. It was a controlled environment. I already had light stringers down there and generators. Everybody was on top of the pile working their way down and if you're working on a machine that's generating hundreds or thousands of cubic feet per minute of exhaust, the Freon would have been displaced anyway—you have a constant flow of oxygen in to where you are—engines can't run without oxygen.

But you couldn't tell that to the DDC. I had to placate them and say, "Okay, I'll talk to the guys about it and we'll get a safety program going."

I brought my own safety people in and I made them orient the guys and we got the program down. I argued the DDC's case for them and won it. But it made me the bad guy because it caused ten guys to go back to their firehouse who wanted to search for victims. But I played ball because it made it easier to go in and out of the area and take people down there and get what I needed done.

Other items being uncovered deep within the pile or in surrounding buildings caused their own issues. Building Six had been occupied by a number of government offices, including U.S. Customs and the Bureau of Alcohol, Tobacco and Firearms; the FBI, CIA, and the Secret Service had space in Building Seven. There were several large bank vaults on the premises belowground, and offices in nearby buildings such as 90 West and 130 Liberty also contained valuables—coin collections, paintings, sports memorabilia. The possibility of looting was a concern from the start, particularly among the construction workers, who feared they'd be blamed for any losses.

CHARLIE VITCHERS

The Port Authority Police Department was in control of property seizures. They were looking for specific artifacts. They sought out all of the gold from the bank vaults, all of the precious metals, silver, anything valuable, all the money in ATM machines. Whatever they knew was in the complex that had a monetary value and could potentially be looted, they went in and got it as soon as it was found or that area could be reached. But sometimes we just came across things. One time a machine tore open a vault that had a couple of million dollars of foreign currency in it, and PAPD bagged it up and collected it. If you found a rifle or a gun or anything, they'd come running over right away. You didn't want to get caught with that in your hand. They would arrest you for it.

I remember one day standing there with my son Charlie, who had started working as a laborer, outside of the Vista Hotel, and there was a grappler digging somewhere in the vicinity. The wind was blowing like crazy and all of a sudden I see $20 bills, $50 bills, $100 bills just blowing across the debris pile.

I said, "Charlie, don't even think about it."

He goes, "Dad, I'm not thinking about it. I don't want any of this shit."

"Just do me a favor," I said. "Don't. I know you won't, but you have to hear this from me. Do not pick anything up on this job site and put it in your pocket."

I didn't see anybody physically breaking into things. I didn't ever see somebody pick something up and put it in their pocket, or walk out of the site with a box under their arm. I did see people in places they had no business being, but I cannot say I ever saw anybody working on the site take anything.

When I went in to evacuate 90 West Street before the pull-down of the South Tower, I had about an hour before the wall was scheduled to be pulled, and I went up to the roof and I worked my way down through the building to make sure it was evacuated and nobody was in there. I got down to the eighteenth floor or the nineteenth floor where it was very unsafe. It had been completely gutted by fire, there were holes in the floor, voids all over the place. And I heard somebody moving around. I walked over to the east side of the building and I saw two women with a guy standing there, handing a fifty-pound safe to another guy.

I asked them what the hell they were doing in the building. They said that they had permission to be there. But at that time there was no security on that building.

I said, "Who are you?"

One woman gave me some name. She said, "I worked here, I'm an accountant. I'm just trying to retrieve some stuff out of my own office."

I said, "You can't be here. We're getting ready to pull down the south side of Tower Two, and if that thing hits the building and nobody knew you were here you'd be killed and we wouldn't even know about it. You have to leave the building. Now."

I bought the story at first, but I was smart enough to get on the radio and asked the police department to stop them for questioning when they left. I later heard they were all arrested. I never saw them again. I didn't care to see them again.

In the Vista Hotel, the safe-deposit boxes were all blown open from the debris collapse—jewelry, watches, cash, wallets, pocketbooks, a lot of valuables just laying on the floor.

I went and got some empty crates and put them out and the guys started picking everything up and started throwing it in the crates—we loaded them up. The Port Authority cops came over, took all of that cash that we found, put it in the back of a Jeep, and drove away with it. Several weeks later we hit cash in Tower One to the tune of like $5 million. The grappler went in and *BOOM*, there were bills all over the place, a lot of foreign money, 20-pound notes floating all over the place. They didn't have enough cops to retrieve it all so we gave them laborers and black garbage bags.

Afterwards it looked like you just raked your lawn. All the garbage bags were sitting out there and every one of them was loaded to the top with bills. Port Authority guys came by with an ambulance or a truck, and a guy with a shoulder mounted camera filming all of the money going in the truck. They weren't looting. They were trying to make sure they weren't accused of looting later on.

But when we found live ammunition that belonged to one of the law enforcement agencies, that could have killed someone, nobody was interested.

WILLIE QUINLAN, IRONWORKER

There was a lot of live ammo. If you hit it with a torch while burning steel, or got too close, the heat would make everything go off. It happened several times. The bullets went off. One guy got hit in the face. In a case like that we would go in and dig all that ammo out and get rid of it in order to make it a safe environment to work in.

CHARLIE VITCHERS

The ironworkers made a big stink out of it. They said, "We're not going back over there unless you guys clean up the ammo." So I called Customs and we had a Customs guy come to a meeting. "Oh yeah," he said. "We'll give you men."

They never showed up. Two days later I finally got a hundred spackle buckets and I gave them to my laborers. I said, "Just start shoveling up the fucking bullets. Put them in the spackle buckets so we can keep working over here."

After we pushed them all to the side and broom swept the deck we started burning again. We found skids of bullets, shotgun shells and 9 millimeters, 380s, skids and skids of bullets.

I called them up and asked, "You guys want your bullets?"

But they didn't. So, the bullets got thrown away. They were taken to Fresh Kills. They ended up in Dumpsters, I kid you not.

As fall turned into winter, there was construction activity everywhere, recovery activity everywhere. The site was fully engaged. To everyone's surprise, the weather, which had been mild through the fall, remained that way. It would snow only a few times in the winter of 2001–2002, never enough to dramatically impact work on the pile, and New York was spared a debilitating cold snap.

In September, the DDC had set a goal to bring the site down to grade, or street level, by December 30, the last day of Giuliani's term. At the time, that seemed to be a fantasy, and to the workers on the pile, it was absolutely meaningless. The efficient removal of material didn't demand a strict vertical progression, and they were far more concerned with making recoveries. Leveling structures simply for the sake of leveling structures to meet a random date served no purpose to either end, and in the minds of many, was actually a pointless distraction that hindered both processes.

Nevertheless, in December there was an intense push from the DDC to make that date.

CHARLIE VITCHERS

The North Tower sat dormant for the longest time. AMEC was only digging out the middle of the Tower, but the façade still stood. There were sticks that went on the north face of the Tower and then three or four sticks on the east side of the Tower. We had built a debris road to take us around behind Tower Two, and we couldn't cut down the North Tower and compromise that road—for a long time that kept us from taking down Tower One.

The last four pieces that came down from Tower One were on the northeast corner. They came down in mid-December. We pulled the north ones down first and then gave the east side a haircut from Greenwich Street.

The demolition of Building Four, the demolition of Building Five, and the pull-down of Building Six happened kind of mysteriously to me. Their demolition never came up at any of the trailer meetings. It was never put on the board as far as dates and demo and methods and means. We weren't even supposed to physically walk in them. They were deemed unsafe.

I didn't even realize those buildings were being demo'd until after the work had started. I came into the site one day through Liberty Street and said, "WOW! What the fuck are they doing here?"

It had all been planned by DH Griffin and the DDC without input at all from us or any other contractor in the trailer. I didn't even know enough in advance to tell people to stay away from that area!

Building Four and Building Five were taken down with a wrecking ball, not like one you'd imagine, a round ball or teardrop, but a block fabricated from one of the core columns from the Towers. The use of a wrecking ball has been banned in New York City since the 1970s. It's too dangerous on a lot of different levels. First, you can't control how the building will fall, and since the crane is attached to the ball, if the building really lets go, it can pull the crane down with it. Second, when you're dropping a wrecking ball on steel, rivets can pop and become bullets. I've seen freak accidents happen on job sites before. Those are the reasons why they banned this type of demolition years ago.

We always tried to take everything down in a controlled way, and with spotters looking for remains. I would have stabilized the building first and then picked it apart with a crane and a man basket, from the top down, then laid the steel on a flatbed and just kept going. They were only nine stories tall. But they took them down with a wrecking ball, without spotters, and a lot of people were concerned that there might have still been human remains in those buildings.

I don't even know where that debris went.

BOBBY GRAY

The operator that used the wrecking ball was out of Connecticut; he was not an operator from our Local. Strictly speaking, from a working point of view, what that man could do with a crane was beyond anything I would ever try. It was crazy, but amazing, pure artistry.

He was using a 4100 crane. A 250-ton machine. I remember I came around the corner on to Church Street and all I saw was the boom just flying through the air. My first thought was, "The boom let go!" I thought something catastrophic had happened. But before I could finish the thought, the boom came back around and I was like, "Huh?"

Then it was gone again and I was like, "What the fuck is going on?" I was ready to go and yank the operator out of the seat. This guy would let go of the ball and get such a reaction through the crane—he was stressing it so much he was getting sparks coming out of the boom pins because he was getting so much movement going through all the different sections, but he was amazing.

The wrecking ball weighed 6,000 pounds.

CHARLIE VITCHERS

The DDC had Building Six pulled down without any input from us. At least they didn't kill anybody. They stuck burners in at night to preburn pieces of that building. I specifically remember nights being on that site and seeing torches in that building and saying, "What the frick are these guys doing?" But they fucked that one up. It took them weeks.

To them, everything was a joke. All they were focusing on was, "How fast can we take this down?" My opinion was that they should have taken them down mechanically, in a controlled way, rather than pulling them down. But they were running the show.

Nobody knew what the plan was. The day when they decided to pull that building down, we didn't find out about it until 9 A.M. It hadn't even been mentioned at the 7 A.M. meeting. I found out about it by walking out and seeing fire trucks with dust suppression hoses ready and all of this stuff going on and I said, "What are they doing?" Someone tells me, "Oh, they're going to try to pull down Building Six."

I walked up around Vesey Street and I saw the grapplers setting up and I asked, "What are you guys doing?"

"We're pulling it down."

The only problem I had with taking those buildings down—Four, Five, and Six—was that they may have come down without being fully searched. By taking them down that way, it made it less likely to find remains. I can't say for sure that there were body parts in those buildings that were not recovered. But we would have never taken those buildings down unless we had proof they had been searched.

Maybe I'm wrong. I'm hoping that I am. Sam says the fire department put guys in that building early, went through and sorted and sifted through all the rubble.

They told me Building Six was completely evacuated before the Towers collapsed, and that Four and Five had been evacuated and everyone accounted for, and I don't doubt that. I'm not concerned about the people that had been working in those buildings. I'm talking about the jumpers from the Towers, and the people that got blown out of the Towers when the planes hit and when the Towers collapsed. Ninety West and 130 Liberty had been evacuated, too, and searched several times, but we found all kinds of body parts—arms and legs and everything—all through those buildings.

I know we had a body come off Building Six way before they decided to demo the building. The fire department went up in a man basket and surveyed the site from the crane. They spotted some body parts on the top of Building Six, and went up and retrieved them.

Some of the firemen who were still missing were last seen going into Six. A personal friend of mine lost her husband down there. He was last seen running back into Building Six to go through the concourse to get into Tower One to help with evacuations. He was never recovered.

When Four, Five, and Six were taken down, the fire department and police were still concentrating on the pile, in the Towers, where they knew they had lost guys. Not that they didn't care, but nobody was making those buildings a part of the agenda at the meetings yet.

Then it just happened. They were gone. I just wonder if anybody ever got a good look at what might have still been in them.

The DDC hit their deadline. By December 31, the bulk of the site was down to grade. A small portion of Building Six was left standing to protect workers laboring on the PATH tunnel from the elements. Hardly a single beam or pile of debris remained above street level.

The fires that had smoldered for more than three months were out. The pillars of smoke that had risen into the air finally dissipated. The slurry wall tieback operation, while still far from complete, was a success. The largest cranes on-site were being dismantled, their work done. Nearly 1 million tons of debris had been removed.

On January 1, Michael Bloomberg was sworn in as mayor of New York, and on January 7, Bovis officially took over as the site's construction manager for the DDC. The estimated number of victims continued to drop, as officials cross-checked lists. Still, more than an estimated 2,300 victims had not been identified. They were still there. Waiting.

CHAPTER NINE

HEROES

In January, as winter set in, the dull sky over Manhattan matched the mood at Ground Zero. Even on the rare days when the sky above Ground Zero burned a bright blue, the pit remained a mire of gray.

The days were beginning to merge, becoming numbingly the same. The workers' eyes, bloodshot with fatigue, sank deep into their skulls. Many were stricken with a hacking cough. Months of relentless seven-day-a-week twelve-hour shifts were beginning to take their toll.

The endless grind of the pile meant that few had had the time to reflect on what they were seeing on a daily basis, about what it meant to labor in a burial ground. All their energy was directed toward the task at hand, to the logistics of deconstruction, to finding a safe and efficient way to simultaneously remove material and assist in recovery efforts without short-changing either charge.

It was during the early weeks of the new year that Charlie Vitchers, Bobby Gray, and others on the pile began to be bothered by a strange disparity. While recovery workers from both the New York Fire Department and Port Authority Police Department retained an acute focus on the recovery of remains, to the construction workers they seemed to be concentrating most of their efforts on locating their own colleagues.

On one level, the construction workers understood. But it still bothered the hell out of them. For just as police and fire personnel felt a special affin-

ity for their fallen uniformed colleagues, the construction workers had developed a similar kinship with the civilians.

Every day, the construction workers overheard police and fire recovery workers talking back and forth in the brusque verbal shorthand that had evolved on the pile. Uniformed victims were referred to as flags, in reference to the American flag that was draped over their bodies before they were carried out of the pit by an honor guard—a ceremony that had been in place, in some form, virtually from the start. Civilians were referred to as bags. They left the pit in body bags or red medical hazmat bags. No flag. No honor guard.

The slight was unintentional but had begun to grate on the workers. As their identification with the civilian victims grew stronger, the construction workers began to take it personally. Emotions long kept in check began to come unhinged.

FATHER BRIAN JORDAN

Construction workers are not accustomed to losing men on the job site or working in an environment where you encounter human remains and bodies. On the rare occasions when they do experience a death on the job, they go to the wake or the funeral, what have you, but they don't have a ritual to deal with death in the same way as the fire and police. Firemen and policemen do die on the job. They had experienced this before. When it happens, they have long-standing rituals that they practice, and the honor guard is one of those rituals.

I think both groups had difficulty understanding the rituals of the other, or in the case of the construction workers, in a sense the lack of a ritual. I think they were all trying to treat the remains with respect and dignity.

BOBBY GRAY

I don't think there was any intentional disrespect towards civilians from fire or police, but there were some flare-ups between construction and uniformed servicemen. To me, if you put a thousand people working in a sandbox together, to think that there weren't going to be problems would be ludicrous. The honor guard was the usual protocol for uniformed services whenever someone dies on duty. So every time they found a body of one of theirs, they would bring down a flag and a priest. For the few minutes it took to carry the body off the pile or out of the pit, everyone would turn off their machine and stop working.

I saw that happen on one of my very first nights down there, right after they recovered a high-ranking fireman. As they brought him out on a stretcher, the firemen lined up and took off their helmets. I was in tears. I didn't feel it was my right to salute, so I just held my hand over my heart.

A lot of guys carried radios to communicate on the pile. Unfortunately, after a body was found, sometimes we'd hear uniformed services ask, "Is it a bag or flag?" so they could form the honor guard if they recovered one of their own. That was really unfortunate. I don't think it was meant in disrespect, but that's the language they used.

Later on, I did start hearing people, construction workers, saying, "This isn't right. Civilians are just as important as uniformed services."

I felt guilty. They were right.

I actually think there were fewer problems between construction workers and other personnel than you'd expect, a whole lot less. In the construction industry, there are a lot of tough guys. I think most of us showed incredible restraint.

CHARLIE VITCHERS

The guys and the girls working construction on the site started saying, "You know, if you're a cop or a fireman you get a flag, if you're a civilian you get a bag." And that's what was happening.

It just evolved out in the pit. During the initial chaos if a body was found it went out on a gurney. It didn't even get a body bag. It just went out and was driven all the way up to the OCME's office.

When the sun finally came out, the fire department recognized that the world was watching them. It seemed like one day all of a sudden every fireman that was found got an honor guard. I remember saying to myself, "Geez look at these guys, they're lining up on the debris roads and they got an ambulance at the top of the hill."

Whenever a fireman or a cop was found, they'd put whatever they found in a small bag, or if it was a whole body, in a full body bag. Then they'd bring the chaplain down. He'd say a prayer at the body and offer a moment of silence or whatever. Then they would put the flag over the gurney and walk it up a debris ramp, like Tully Road. It originally involved just a handful of firemen. Ten or fifteen guys would line up on the hill. They would walk the body up. They'd get the salute. They'd put the body in the ambulance and drive it to the OCME's office.

Civilians, on the other hand, were usually put in red bags and set on the side. The bags sometimes sat there a couple of hours until they found enough to make it worth the run up to the morgue, because very few civilians were found intact. The firemen got the honor guard out of there, and the civilians would be in red medical evidence bags, not even body bags, and taken out in the back of these John Deere mules.

A lot of the construction workers simply thought that it wasn't right, morally, that some people got a "flag" and some people got a "bag." A real bad attitude started to form down there over that. Construction workers would say to me, "Ah, the cops and fire department only give a fuck about finding their own."

Not everybody had that attitude, but the mood was there. At the same time, we hadn't asked for anything to be done about it.

Our biggest pet peeve down there became, "Treat these civilians like they are victims of a war. Because they are."

FDNY, PAPD, and NYPD saw the honor guard issue from a completely different perspective. They didn't intend to slight civilians and didn't feel as if they were. Both groups are organized along military lines, and the honor guard is a ceremony rooted in traditional military protocol for service veterans. They weren't doing less for civilians by following established protocol for their own members.

Both groups were completely oblivious to the mood growing among construction workers on the pile. The issue came to a climax one day in January in an incident involving grappler operator Pia Hofmann.

PIA HOFMANN, OPERATING ENGINEER

Why I reacted the way I did was because I and everybody else on that site—every other construction worker—had witnessed the fact that finding firefighters and police was so much more important to them. And as far as the civilians, it was like, "Oh, okay we got somebody here. Bring the bag, bring the gator, get them out of here." And it was wrong, totally wrong. But nobody really said anything. They just watched it happen.

We had been digging in one area for days. We knew there was a body. We knew we were close. We could smell it. I was working with the firefighters and I went for coffee. I come back from coffee and start digging again and the chief comes up and tells me, and not very nice either, "You got to stop digging over here. I think we found a body."

I'm saying to myself, "Like I don't already know that?"

I got a little upset. That was my first civilian. A female. Everybody else that I had dug up were all firefighters or police.

At first I didn't say anything. Everybody was afraid to say anything. But at that point I really didn't care. I was not down there to make friends.

So I said, "What is it? A uniformed officer? Or is it just a civilian?"

He says, "Oh, we think it's just a civilian."

With this I threw my hands up in the air and I said, "Oh, I guess that means I can go back to work in no time because all you're gonna do is get the bag, shove the civilian in there, and get her the hell out of here, right?" He gave me the dirtiest look and started to walk away.

I said, "Let me tell you something. You're not moving this body until I say you move this body and until you get a priest down here. I want a priest, I want the flag and I want an honor guard."

Now a whole bunch of ironworkers were right there and a bunch of laborers and they were all standing around and giving me thumbs-up.

This firefighter, he just walks away.

CHARLIE VITCHERS

Pia was very emotional, and very tied to the recoveries emotionally. She wanted it all done in a dignified way. I'd go down to bum cigarettes off of her because I would hear rumors that she was getting out of control. I'd get on her grappler and I'd open the door, I'd say, "Give me a cigarette."

She'd go, "Oh, you and your fucking cigarettes. You *never* have fucking cigarettes."

Of course I had a pack of cigarettes. I just wanted to talk to her. When the incident happened with the civilian, Pia actually opened up the grappler jaws and brought it down around the body. She didn't crush it into the ground, but put the jaws on either side gently, protecting it. "You aren't getting near this thing," she said. "I want a fuckin' priest down here *now*." She didn't want that body moved until a priest came down. She wanted a flag put over the body, and the body taken out of the job site like they were doing for their own.

She was right, you know? And everybody got it.

BOBBY GRAY

She was not going to let that body go. The recovery was a woman's body. I was actually at lunch and I got a phone call saying, "Pia's losing it." And I was as much concerned about her as anybody on the crew. So I ran over there thinking that maybe this is the recovery that puts her over the edge. She was very calm, very collected. But determined. She goes, "I want a priest and I want someone to bring a flag. I want this done right."

PIA HOFMANN, OPERATING ENGINEER

I got what I wanted. They called in the priest, they got the flag, the construction workers formed an honor guard, and I was happy. I went back to work. It was like a victory for me.

That night and the next day people that I didn't even know kept coming up to me and shaking my hand and saying, "That was a really great thing you did."

Nobody had ever spoken up before. I guess maybe I'm mad at myself for not having voiced my opinion sooner, but this was my first civilian recovery.

CHARLIE VITCHERS

A few days later I went to a morning meeting at the OEM's office. I thought that was a perfect opportunity to make a request in front of everybody that the civilians be handled and treated with an honor guard the same way the cops and the firemen were doing it.

I sat in the meeting and I don't even think I heard what was going on because I was just focused on how I was going to stand up in this room and change the subject, that's what I had to do.

But I chickened out. I didn't get up and I didn't say what I was gonna say.

I finally got my balls too late. I followed the guys from the fire department and police department out the door and said, "Guys, can I talk to you for a minute? I was gonna bring this up inside but I think it's something we can probably settle among ourselves without making a big stink. The guys in the field who are helping you guys doing recoveries want an honor guard for the civilians, the same way you are treating your own."

The guys from the fire department turned around and said immediately, "We don't have a problem with that at all. If you guys have been feeling that all along you guys should have said something to us earlier, you really should have. Why didn't someone say something earlier? We don't have a problem with that."

That really blew me away. After I got back to the site the cops got back to me and it was an immediate "Yes" from them too. That was it. The request was granted.

Now I had to find construction workers to carry the gurney because the cops and the firemen weren't gonna carry up the gurney of the civilian, but they agreed to form an honor guard for us. We didn't want that anyway. We wanted the construction workers to carry it up.

We also wanted an ambulance at the top of the hill for all of the bodies we found. The decision filtered down to Lt. John Ryan of the PAPD in the field later that afternoon. Ryan told me he heard what was going on, and he didn't have any problem with it, but he also told me, "If anybody finds a civilian, you guys better have your act together and find people that want to carry the gurney up right away because we're not gonna wait around."

My son Charlie was working for me down in the pit. He found it very tough down there, but he got through it. I told him, "If you have to bail out any time, it's not a problem." But he dealt with it very well and was my right-hand man for a while.

I kind of put Charlie in charge, but we didn't find any civilians that afternoon. At the 5:30 P.M. meeting I announced to the guys in the trailer that from now on when we find civilians, we're forming an honor guard. I described the protocol. I said, "When a civilian is found I'll need volunteers. I need names now. Write your name on a list."

Everybody in that room said they'd be honored, from laborers to Jim Tully, the president of Tully Construction. In fifteen minutes, I had dozens of signatures and by the end of the day I had hundreds more.

When I left that night I told my son Charlie, "Listen. You're the guy. You have to orchestrate this and make it happen. When they find the first civilian, get a hold of John Ryan, get a hold of Stevie, Sam, or Mike, and pick the names off the list. Whoever's down in the pit, grab them. When the cops or the firemen find a civilian, you make sure you immediately get guys to the bottom of the ramp to get ready to take the gurney up the hill."

I was off the next day. I finally had to get out of there. I don't know how many days I had worked in a row and I needed a break.

So I left the site. I just wanted to get the hell out of there and go up to Pennsylvania and unload. I was driving up Route 80 and my Nextel goes off. It was Charlie. He was crying. I pulled off to the side of the road and he said, "Hey, Dad. We found a civilian."

I could hear it in my son's voice that he was upset, his voice was quivering. I sat there talking to him, trying to calm him down and realizing that I'm getting upset emotionally, too. Because I wished I was there.

CHARLIE VITCHERS, JR., LABORER

When they found the first body I went running around looking for people that I knew. I don't remember why, but a lot of people just weren't there. Whether they were on a break or whatever, I don't know. They just weren't there and I had to find them.

CHARLIE VITCHERS

My son was real upset because someone from the fire department had just told him that if he didn't have six guys at the bottom of that ramp in, like, five minutes, they were gonna put the body in a mule and take it to the OCME's office. I almost turned around but I was already an hour out of the city and I ain't making it back there in five minutes to knock this guy on his ass.

So I say to Charlie, "Relax. So the guys aren't there at the bottom of the ramp, they're not gonna take the body up in a mule. Get ahold of Jim Tully or call whoever's in charge down there and put him on the phone. Let them know what the hell is going on and get back to me and let me know what's going on."

Charlie gets off the phone with me and I'm still hanging on the road. He gets right back on about two minutes later and goes, "It's a laborer."

I said, quietly, "What do you mean it's a laborer?"

He goes, "The civilian we found is a laborer. They found his wallet with him." He was a union laborer who'd been working at the Trade Center on September 11.

My son Charlie's a Local 79 laborer. It was very significant to the union workers that were down there, whether they were ironworkers or whatever, that this guy was a member of a construction union, a brother. We felt the same way the fire department felt when they found one of their brothers, or the police department when they found one of their brothers. What's more significant than finding one of your brothers to be in the first honor guard carried up and out of the hill?

BOBBY GRAY

I'll never forget that. Never. We were down by the North Tower, and it was raining. It was just an ugly day, pouring rain. And we uncovered the first construction worker and he was fairly intact, you could definitely recognize it was a construction worker. The construction workers actually took the boy out and uniformed services lined up for *us*. Normally the procedure was, we would stop what we were doing and get on line and they would bring the flag-draped remains of the uniformed service person through. We thought that was pretty nice when they stopped for us.

I know in my heart that civilians gave their lives to save others. I know there were acts of heroism amongst civilians on the upper floors. Whether you wore a uniform or a skirt that day, it didn't make any difference.

CHARLIE VITCHERS, JR., LABORER

I don't think anyone had any idea that the uniformed guys would line up for us. Everyone kind of felt like they were opposed to a civilian honor guard, but they weren't. One of them even told me, "These guys are every bit as deserving as anyone else." I remember helping to carry the body up the ramp, looking at the flag, and thinking, "This is me, right here. This is a person, this is a human being just like me who had no clue that this was going to happen to them and there was nothing they could do about it."

CHARLIE VITCHERS

They managed to pull it off, they got the people and they got it done. I sat there on the side of the road, and I cried like a baby for probably ten minutes.

These are the memories that suck, you know?

From then on, if we found a civilian and you were there, you wanted to help carry it up. We only needed six or eight people to carry a gurney, and ten guys would want to help. I think it boosted the morale for the construction workers because now we all felt unified with everybody else down there.

As the ceremonies became more and more common, the crowds became larger on the bridge. Instead of just five or ten guys, now you had seventy-five guys on each side of the bridge. Cops, firemen, civilians, everybody mixing, joining the salute for the walk up the hill.

It was a very good thing. It made everyone think, "Why are we here, boys?" This job isn't just "rip and tear." If it was I could have emptied that pit in another month and a half. But that was not why we were there.

There was a point soon after that where they found like maybe six or seven civilians in a row, digging them out so fast that they were putting them in the body bags, putting them in the gurney, putting the flag over them, and then stacking them under the bridge, just stacking these bodies under the bridge because they were still digging more out so fast. So now we had to find twenty-four guys to stop work to come down and carry four or five or six gurneys up the hill.

One time I grabbed all the head honchos. I went up there with Jim Tully, and the lead super from AMEC, and Peter Rinaldi from the Port Authority, one of the engineers from LERA, Lou

Mendes from the DDC—everybody. I'll never forget walking that gurney up the hill, putting it in an ambulance, and looking at Jim Tully. He's teary eyed; I'm teary eyed. You'd say to yourself, "This is why I'm here. This is what it's all about."

After being there that many months and having this happen so suddenly, it reaffirmed your commitment to what you were doing. Let me tell you, after walking that body up the hill and putting it into an ambulance, man, you really sat back and you felt as if it was day one again.

If you save somebody's life, you're a hero, but after September 11 nobody saved anybody's life down there. It's that simple. We collected lives that were already lost. That doesn't make you a hero.

The heroes are the people that died. Heroes die in the end, you know?

CHAPTER TEN

THE BRIDGE

A corner had been turned. Since September 11, lower Manhattan had been defined by the carnage bounded by West Street, Vesey, Liberty, and Church. That was no longer true. Residents had begun to move back into the neighborhood. A scattering of stores, shops, restaurants, and bars had reopened. The West Side Highway was cleared; once it was resurfaced, it would be opened to local traffic. Plans were being drawn up to reopen the PATH tubes and the 1 and 9 subway lines. Normal life was starting to elbow its way back in.

In the pit, recovery continued. Only two major debris piles remained— the sub-grade remnants of Building Six on the northwest corner of the site and the debris from the South Tower that supported Tully Road. They were close, very close to the end.

The last and final phase of the cleanup was to build a bridge nearly 500 feet long that would stretch from the lowest level of the pit up to the street. Trucks and other machinery would no longer have to snake their way along the narrow debris ramp—a ramp many feared still held human remains. Large enough to accommodate two-way traffic, the new bridge would speed debris removal over the final months. And Tully Road finally could be searched for victims whose bodies remained buried in the pile.

For the first time since the attacks, something new would be built. Engineers would design again. Superintendents would set schedules and deadlines. Cranes would move steel, carpenters build forms, and concrete workers pour concrete. With backward serendipity, the construction workers at Ground Zero finally were tasked with doing what they do best: building.

Eyes long trained to look downward began to look up, toward the future.

PETER RINALDI, PORT AUTHORITY, ENGINEER

By January we were getting into fine-tuning because we had quite a bit of the site recovered. The whole cleanup and recovery went much quicker than we had envisioned. Part of that was due to the demeanor and attitude of all the people working at the site. Everyone was there with a purpose, and I think that made things move quicker than on a normal kind of a job.

On the Liberty Street end of the site we were down to grade, the B-6 level, the bottom of the pit. We started planning to build the bridge and were working our way north, getting down to grade.

RICHARD GARLOCK, ENGINEER

We needed a road that could accommodate traffic going into the pit and out of it. But it wasn't immediately obvious how to go about it. A couple of engineering solutions were put on the table. One was a backfill bridge, a soil bridge. Given my sensitivity to the backfilling issue and that it was never a solution that made people happy from the recovery side, some of us were advocating for a structural bridge, so we wouldn't have to put in dirt that would be cross-contaminated. One idea was to build it with existing sub-grade columns. The foundations were in good shape and we thought we could get down to them and reattach columns. In the end, by making use of a prefab bridge, the sequence of debris removal would be simpler.

PETER RINALDI, PORT AUTHORITY, ENGINEER

The area we were using to access the site, Tully Road, was rather large. The fire and the police departments knew there were victims still buried there because they had made some recoveries adjacent to it. The core of Tower Two was a kind of lobby area and they knew that they lost some people there. We had promised the police and the fire department that we would get them into that area. There was a hope that we would find hundreds more people.

We finally came up with the idea of using a prefabricated, temporary bridge, built by a company called Acrow, a Bailey Bridge type of structure. As we were looking at that bridge and laying it out and figuring out how we were going to build a span, we had to consider where the PATH train tracks were going to be rebuilt. We laid out the foundations and the piers for that bridge to avoid the tracks, so when the train and subway tracks were rebuilt, the bridge could stay during any reconstruction on the site. We decided to put it just off to the side of the western edge of Tully Road, heading north down from Liberty Street.

CHARLIE VITCHERS

Temporary bridges like that are usually used on highway projects, to replace an old bridge before you put in a new, permanent one. Acrow supplied the bridge and worked very closely with us. They were very proud to be involved. Their workers at the plant even punched out and worked overtime on their own time to get it done for us.

The task of building the bridge was basically mine. I worked out delivery with Acrow and the actual installation and construction of the bridge with the ironworkers. The schedule of the bridge going in was dictated by the recovery set with the fire department and the police department, because the completion of that bridge marked the completion of the rest of the debris removal, starting beneath the Tully Road. I knew that by the time the bridge was finished the only thing that we would have to concentrate on was Tully Road. There were a lot of people missing over there. And that was the spot everybody wanted to get to.

It was the beginning of the end, absolutely.

The installation of the bridge led to the realization that the job would soon be over. An undercurrent of anxiety began to spread, not just among workers on the site, but among all those involved with the cleanup. Institutionally, the reactions varied wildly. The DDC started a more aggressive monitoring of men and equipment, and the Port Authority began to push to reclaim administrative authority over the Trade Center site. Predictably, the individuals on the ground—the construction and recovery workers—resisted. Until the last spadeful of debris was searched, they weren't about to submit to directives that did not prioritize the recovery of victims.

CHARLIE VITCHERS

When the bridge was going in, all of a sudden everything was happening. People were yelling and screaming. All these different groups just started going nuts. At the time a lot of firemen were saying, "Well, the cops are just trying to slow the fucking job down. And I'd say to the firemen, "Well, you guys are trying to slow the fucking job down, too." The worst thing that happened on that site was Sammy got sick and left. Everybody thought he had a heart attack. In the end it turned out that he didn't, he was fine, but he left the site in March.

Sammy was very, very important to the job down there. He had everyone's respect. Sammy would make a decision on your behalf if you explained it and it made sense, even if he had to shelve what he wanted to do.

When Sammy left, some people tried to take advantage. It was just that simple. Mike and Steve remained and did a great job, but they didn't quite have Sammy's personality. The agencies, the DDC, everybody tried to take advantage because now they thought they could go rip shit down.

Sammy would have just said, "No, we want to search for remains," and that would have been it. But after Sammy left nobody was on the same page until I could bring Mike and Steve up to speed about our plans.

The DDC relocated into Three World Financial, the AmEx Building, and took the entire thirtieth and thirty-first floors. Whatever the date was that they moved in, that was the date it got worse for us. Because now we had all these executives, with window views, looking directly down on to Ground Zero, micromanaging.

I used to get calls: "Put that water truck on the other side of the site. There's too much dust up here." Meanwhile, this guy's trying to help suppress dust where he already is. They can't see that because they were 400 feet away.

I always tried to have a machine on standby near a recovery to work with the fire department. The operator might be running a machine somewhere else, but I could always send him back to the idle machine when he was needed. All the operator would have to do is walk back to the machine. The firemen were okay with that.

But accountability for the equipment became my biggest headache. If a machine wasn't moving, I'd get a phone call from guys looking out the window with binoculars on the thirtieth floor of Three World Financial. Somebody would be screaming, "Why isn't that machine moving? That hasn't moved in a half an hour. There's nobody in the machine, Charlie!"

And I'd say, "Well how do you know that?"

"Because I'm looking at it," they'd say.

So I'd tell them, "Well, the guy went to take a leak. He'll be back in ten minutes." Because I knew if I told them the machine was idle, they'd go nuts.

That was the kind of craziness that was happening down there.

People like that very rarely go on to a construction site and get their boots dirty. If they did, they wouldn't survive for very long. You can't belittle and act condescending to people who aren't going to put up with it. And construction people don't put up with that shit. To a construction worker, if you're wearing a suit and a tie, you're probably an idiot. That's why when owners show up on building sites, the workers disappear. They don't want to be standing there because if an owner talks to the wrong person on the site and says the wrong thing, that worker is just going to say, "Hey, that isn't my fucking job."

Then the owner will want him fired.

• • •

It wasn't just the DDC who were throwing their weight around. The role of the PAPD—or at least the role the PAPD wanted—also began to change, further altering the work dynamic in the pit.

CHARLIE VITCHERS

The fire department had basically been in charge of the recovery and I think that bothered the PAPD. They took it personally and in the pit there was a lot of animosity between the firemen and the PAPD. Over time it became pronounced. PAPD's attitude was "Why does the fire department have more guys than we do in here?" And the fire department wondered why PAPD had so many men.

I think PAPD felt they weren't getting recognized because they "only" lost 37 guys. We knew they lost 37 guys. We also knew the fire department lost 343 and NYPD lost 23, and at that time we still thought there were 4,000 or so civilians missing out there.

I don't care—one guy lost was one too many, and if they had lost 500, 500 was too many. My attitude was "Let's get together and move on and get the job done." But the cops felt like they were getting pushed out, so they pushed back by claiming, "It's our house," because the Trade Center had been operated by the Port Authority. So they had their own little rivalry. It was just stupid because the Port Authority Police had always been involved in recoveries. But all of a sudden they were trying to do more than that. They had always been in charge of security, but now that we were getting near the end they came in with all this protocol.

They gave everybody the typical boilerplate Port Authority employee application as if we were all employees of Port Authority. They wanted everybody to give them their Social Security number and the right to look into their financial and criminal background. None of the guys had a problem with the criminal history, but a lot of guys had personal reasons why they didn't feel they needed to divulge their bank accounts to the Port Authority.

It got laughed off the table. The unions backed up the construction workers and we all said, "Screw you."

There had always been something of a rift between the firemen and cops down there, too, and that got worse. The fact that the cops always wore guns down there was a big issue with the fire department. Why did a cop digging on a pile need to be carrying a sidearm? The firemen would bust them about it and say things like, "Are you afraid of being robbed or something? What are you going to do, shoot somebody?"

There was always some flack between those two particular agencies. That's just the way they are. They do not get along. The firemen took the position that they were in charge of recovery, and that was that. PAPD wanted their spotters on the pile, too. You couldn't argue with that; PAPD lost thirty-seven guys and felt they had the right to be there to look for their own. Like everybody else, the job really affected them. They were just as emotionally attached to what they saw and did as anybody. But then again, did all the civilian families that lost people have the right to be down there digging, too? Who could say who was right and who was wrong?

Towards the end, after things had been running smooth, they came in like gangbusters and started telling us we're not doing the "right thing," we weren't digging in the right places and looking for "their guys." Way late in the game when we were excavating the Tully Road and under Building Six they started complaining about our procedures and the kind of equipment we were using, the whole approach we had taken around the whole site since day one of the tieback operation. All of a sudden they didn't like it. We'd been using buckets to peel up floor slabs and now they wanted us to use grapplers, which would just rip and tear. If there was any forensic evidence, using the grapplers would just pulverize it. It didn't make any sense and it put us on edge.

Finally just to save from arguing, I gave in. We switched the bucket back to a grappler. The grappler operator was cursing because now he's just ripping and ripping and ripping, trying to get this stuff up. If there was any forensic evidence in there, all he was doing was pulverizing it.

Then PAPD backed off and said, "Put the buckets back on."

We put the buckets back on and we started peeling up. We ended up pulling seventy people out of there. If we would have kept going with the grapplers I don't know if we would have found everybody.

And every day there was somebody from the Port Authority Police Department giving a snippy opinion to some reporter as to what was going on in the job site. Guys would ask me, "Did you see the *Post* today?"

I'm like, "No, what's in the *Post*?"

"Well the Port Authority Police are saying this and saying this and saying this and saying this."

We were all told that we can't talk to the media. I was told through Bovis, "You're not to talk to the media. You do not let cameras in. If you see anybody, report it to the PAPD and these people will be escorted off of the site." If anybody shouldn't have been talking to the media, it was PAPD, so there was some animosity down there over that.

The approaching end had a different but no less dramatic effect on the men and women still working in the pit. With vast areas of the foundation floor cleared of debris, it was possible for grappler operators to spread material out on the B-6 level so teams of firefighters and police officers could rake through the debris looking for remains. But as that task became easier from a logistical standpoint, on a personal level it became more difficult. Until the very end, everyone on-site held out hope that somewhere deep within the pile, hundreds of bodies lay awaiting discovery. That didn't happen.

As it became more and more apparent that there were to be no mass recoveries, searching became an obsession. The recovery process stalled as the same debris was searched again and again.

CHARLIE VITCHERS

After the bridge was in, we had the ability to run trucks much faster than we had over the first six months. But there were times when we went weeks and nothing much was found. When they did find remains, there wasn't any flesh to speak of. They were just finding bone fragments.

What would happen is, we had spotters working with the machinery down in the pit. If they saw anything, they pulled it out immediately. But if they didn't see anything, we put the debris in a drop zone. Then we spread it out and the recovery guys raked through it.

This is getting towards the end. Whenever anyone from either police or fire was looking for remains, all it took for either the cops or the firefighters to want another look is for one guy to say, "We didn't look at that."

That was fine with me. I might have known that a pile had already been searched by the cops, but if a firefighter didn't think it was fully searched, I'd say, "You guys want to rake it out again because you don't think that they looked at it good enough? Fine."

And vice versa.

We didn't complain about it. We understood that this was the reality of the situation down here and boys will be boys. So let's just play. Let's do what we can to make it go away, so that the debris pile can be put on a truck and sent to Staten Island and we don't have to worry about it again.

We weren't going to move any faster just because we had the ability to move faster, all right? It was gonna take what it was gonna take.

I remember the last couple of weeks when all we had was that one big pile of debris in front of Building Six. The rest of the site had been cleaned right down to the track beds for the PATH trains. We removed the gravel in the track beds and we ripped up all of the asphalt grindings that we had put down on top of already searched areas for ramps. We even let them rake and search through all that, just in case something fell out of the truck, over and above what they even requested.

The fire department would tell me, "We signed off on that pile, Charlie, don't worry about it." But they hadn't. Or the cops hadn't. Not officially. We were keeping track of it all on a grid, declaring areas clean and searched and free of debris. Every time we hit the B-6 level and were scraping concrete, we hosed it down, broomed it, and covered every inch of it with 12 by 12-inch timber pontoonlike decking, so that we all knew anywhere that was covered by pontoons had been searched. You know, some people didn't even want that.

I said, "Well, it's either that, or we're gonna be walking in 12 to 14 inches of water and muck every day. There's water down there. We have to keep draining it. But if we can't keep up with the draining, we've got to put timber pontoons down to maintain a dry surface."

So they said, "Okay. Fine. Let's call Oregon and tell them to start cutting down trees." You know, it was a joke to them.

I said, "Well, I don't care how much money you spend. But, this is the only way it's gonna work."

It took a while, but then truck after truck after truck from Oregon just started showing up. And we managed to lay timber on that whole deck.

I wanted to make sure I had everything covered. You could feel the tension in the searchers, the fire department and the police department. If they weren't satisfied with an area, they weren't going to leave that area and move on. So it was very important to me to hit the B-6 level, broom sweep the slab, have the fire department look at it, agree that it's clean, that there's nothing left to search for, then let's cover it up. Now we can use that area as either a storage area or a rake area.

Even when it got down to the end of the job, the cops and the firemen said, "We're not sending the pontoons off to the dump. We want the pontoons to go to Staten Island. We want them chipped up and we want them looked at again."

They wanted to make sure that nothing at all, not even a tooth or something, had somehow gotten stuck in the pontoon.

I said, "Fine. If that's what you want me to do, then that's what we'll do." And that's what we did.

I didn't want someone to tell me six months later they wanted the whole thing broom swept again because they think we might find an earring. I wasn't going to go back and say I left a stone unturned. I just wanted to make sure that we satisfied everyone, that we had searched every inch of that sixteen acres.

To the construction workers on the site, the recovery of victims remained the sole objective, a moral imperative. Yet, they rarely learned whether a particular set of remains had been identified, or the name of the victim, or where they lived, or who they loved, or who missed them and was waiting for them to be found. Apart from the families of those they had known personally, the construction workers had very little formal contact with victims' families. It wasn't their role, and few families were pressing to meet the workers.

One day in April, all of that changed for Charlie Vitchers when Andrea Haberman's father made his way into the Bovis trailer.

CHARLIE VITCHERS

Jack Mesagno, our project manager, said to me, "Some guy's here to see you. We think that you should talk to him. He's here with his wife and his sister. We told him that you're the guy he should really talk to. They lost their daughter or something."

It was the weirdest thing—I'm thinking to myself, "How did this guy get this far in?" And now he's in my trailer.

GORDON HABERMAN, FATHER

My daughter Andrea was an employee of Carr Futures in Chicago. She flew in to New York on September 10 for what was to be a three-day stay in New York. Carr Futures had an office on the ninety-second floor of the North Tower. It was the first business trip of her career. She was twenty-five years old.

She'd been in the Tower only about forty-five minutes before the first plane hit. She was on the phone with a coworker. That was the only proof we had she was there.

Back in Wisconsin, we were frantic. We drove to New York and were one of the first cars allowed back across the Holland Tunnel.

Carr Futures set up a room at the Waldorf-Astoria that was open twenty-four hours a day for the families. My wife and I hit the bricks in Manhattan and visited thirty-two medical centers, looking for my daughter. Part of me still doesn't believe it happened.

We were back in New York in April of 2002 to meet with the other families from Carr, reconnecting with people we had met before. People flew in from all over the world. There had been an informational meeting earlier that morning with the FBI and Justice Department. They had found nothing of Andrea at that point.

A room for families that overlooked the site had been set up on the twentieth floor of Liberty Plaza. It was strictly for family members of victims, a very emotional room.

My wife, Kathy, and my sister and I were looking down at the trailers and the workers on-site. From up above, the scope of the work was amazing. I watched these guys working in the pit for hours, raking the debris at the bottom and cutting steel. I knew none of them would ever walk away from this cleanly—none of us will.

I wanted to know these guys. I needed to know what type of people were looking for my daughter. I needed to know. Who was looking for Andrea? How were they doing it? How could they keep doing this? How were they able to do this with some kind of decency?

We determined then that we needed to talk to somebody on the site. We wanted to thank people.

There happened to be a chaplain on duty in the room. We started talking with him and he explained to us what all the trailers were. When I told him I wanted to meet someone, the chaplain told us we should find this guy named Charlie Vitchers.

The site was still blocked off, but we went down the elevator and just started walking through barriers across the street. We were stopped a couple times by police. We told them that we wanted to find a Charlie Vitchers and thank the workers. They kept saying, "You can't do that, you can't go in." Finally a Port Authority police officer told us, "Go ahead."

We started working our way past those trailers and walked into one and said we were trying to locate Charlie Vitchers. They sent us to another trailer, then another one, and then we found ourselves in the Bovis trailer.

He came out and we were very emotional. We told him thanks. Then I said, "Please find our daughter." I remember my wife was crying. He told us they would do their best.

He didn't have to see us. He didn't have to meet with us. He was probably wondering, "How in heck did they get on-site?" But there we were.

CHARLIE VITCHERS

They were real upset. Andrea hadn't been found or identified yet and they felt that they weren't going to go home with anything. I figured they wanted a piece of something from the site and they wanted to get permission from somebody who would give them something, a little piece of steel, some glass, anything.

They had every opportunity to pick something up on their way in, to put it in their pocket and run, but Gordon wasn't that kind of a guy.

I talked to his family for a while, and while I was talking I had one of the ironworkers burn a piece of metal. He made a small cross out of steel and I gave it to him.

The guy practically fainted. He had to sit down, he was really upset and started crying. I told him, "We will find your daughter. You've got to give it time. We'll do our best."

GORDON HABERMAN, FATHER

Before we left, Charlie gave us his cell phone number.

We walked off the site and just sat crying on the curb in front of St. Paul's Church. It was a pretty emotional meeting for us.

From that point on our lives changed. A remarkable friendship began with Charlie. Every subsequent visit to New York has involved getting together with Charlie. We weren't New Yorkers. We weren't with other victims' family members all the time who have access in New York or can discuss this with each other. But what we do have is Charlie. And every time we have come back to New York, we have Charlie. He'll tell us what he knows about what has been going on. Through the process, this friendship with Charlie has blossomed.

He has introduced us to ironworkers and so many other construction workers. Now every time we go back to New York for a 9/11 family meeting or memorial or other event, we have a reunion of sorts with these guys. The people we have met since then, the people Charlie has exposed us to, have put a human side to this carnage. They have literally put their arms around us and helped us in ways we don't even understand.

I call them "the guys." I have their pictures on our refrigerator. These are "you and me" type people, they were thrust into this situation by circumstances. How could one not be impacted by this?

These guys were given this task. To call it a job is ridiculous— what they did wasn't in a job description, they just took it. They've become very important to us. I hope in the long-term that they are all okay, that someday I can do something for them, and can give them thanks.

Many people don't understand, but this isn't over for any of us. The only positive I can take from any of it are the associations and the friendships. I cherish that. Ordinary people like Charlie and the guys that helped get us through.

They've had such a calming comforting effect on us. It's so hard to explain. From a family member's perspective, Charlie and the ironworkers and the others have been such a source of comfort—it's hard to even use that word and reconcile it with the atrocity. But speaking for the families, to know there were good people, normal people looking for our daughters and sons and husbands and wives has been such a source of comfort. The government wasn't doing this—this was being done by regular guys.

It is very important people understand what the construction workers did. Like I said, no one walked away from this clean. They found 19,000 body parts. I've met Father Jordan, and he told me, "I saw God in the work of these people." That helps and continues to help. Charlie continues to help. What they've given us is hard to articulate in words.

In May of 2002, a month after we met Charlie, a sheriff came to our house in Wisconsin and informed us they found the first piece of Andrea.

CHAPTER ELEVEN

LAST COLUMN

How would they leave? How would it end? When the construction workers talked about the job among themselves, most referred to their time at Ground Zero as "the worst and the best" job they had ever had. Just as work on the original construction of the Trade Center had come to represent the best of New York's construction industry a generation before, the work at Ground Zero would serve as a similar milestone. But it was far more personal.

Despite all the sweat and horror and tears, many wondered how they could walk away from the only job in their lives that had mattered so much. Despite all they had learned about themselves and one another during the previous months, as the end came into sight the answer to that question remained elusive.

Like so much else at Ground Zero, the answers would come from within—from the pit itself.

JIM ABADIE, BOVIS

Towards the end of the job it wasn't a crisis anymore and there wasn't any emergency. Meetings with the DDC that once had taken place twice a day got down to once a week. I started going down to the pit just once a day for a couple of hours, maybe hit one of the morning meetings or afternoon meetings.

It was more, "Let's punch list this job and go on to the next one," clean up this area or move this street pole over here or that street pole over there. I had a lot more time, personally, to detach from the site. But some of the guys there . . . a lot of the workers became infatuated with it in almost an unhealthy way. They were going, "I've got to work another twelve hours, I've got to get this, I've got to do this." And really, the only thing they were doing was moving a pile of steel that's already been searched or restripping a street.

There was no reason anymore why somebody had to work more than five days a week. But some guys would never leave. It became more important than it really was.

They had a great team. No one down there had ever had a job where people worked together for such a common purpose. On a regular job, the biggest purpose is to get it done. But really, it's to make money so they could go home to their families and hang out with their friends. But on this job everybody shared the goal of getting it finished. That was really true for the first four or five months of the job.

After that there was no need. After a while—I don't know if this is the right word—but it almost became a sickness, it was unhealthy. The only way I can describe it, I guess, is like post-traumatic stress syndrome or whatever they call it.

When this thing finally ended and everybody had to leave, a lot of guys just never left. You know, some guys never left Vietnam and some guys never left the Gulf War; there will be a bunch of guys that will never leave Iraq. It's the same. This was a war zone.

BOBBY GRAY

I think a lot of people were just so tuned in to what we were doing there, we knew it was going to be a hard thing to leave our world. Towards the end the atmosphere was starting to get a little bit lighter. We weren't finding mass graves or lots of remains. It had slowed down and I think there was a little bit of light, you know. It was May, and June was around the corner and the weather was getting warm and your life was starting to get warm again. The biggest fear became leaving all of these people.

HOLLY VITCHERS

I know most of the construction workers that Charlie worked with. Over time I would go down there and meet him if they were going somewhere after work or whatever. I went to a lot of the memorial services and I started to get to know the guys. And I know that a lot of them had troubles at home.

Because they didn't talk to their people. They just kind of shut it up inside. A lot of them are really damaged from working down there, emotionally. They couldn't let it go. When it came time to start pulling people out of there when it was getting towards the end, people would make excuses not to leave. "Charlie, I need to do this, I need to do that." They almost made jobs for themselves to stay there.

It was a very emotional connection down there. People were very connected to the site. Charlie was, too. Charlie was, too, for sure.

CHARLIE VITCHERS

I think all the searching at the end was psychological. Most of the people down there knew by the end of March that we could probably sift through and rake that stuff and get it off the site in three weeks' time and that was it, we're done. Instead, it went another eight weeks.

Guys just didn't want to leave the site. People could not deal with the end coming, with being told they're being reassigned. Guys had been down there for seven months and all of a sudden they saw that in two weeks they could be out of there. So it was, "No, let's keep looking at the debris again," and again and again and again and again, which is fine. Nobody told me they couldn't. I didn't have a personal interest in staying there or leaving.

Me, I just wanted to make sure that when I walked out of there I left no stone unturned, that I knew I had done everything I could and I could go home and fall asleep at night. Maybe there are the people today that have to look at themselves in the mirror and deal with the "what ifs." Maybe they failed to do the right thing when they were expected to do the right thing.

I don't have to do that.

Everybody—FDNY, PAPD, NYPD, the DDC, the mayor, the construction workers, crane operators, ironworkers—began to sense that their work had taken on a genuine symbolism. The rapidly emptying pit was evidence that in spite of all the death and destruction wrought on September 11, America had come back. In a war on terror that had yet to be fully engaged, the conclusion of the cleanup and recovery at Ground Zero was the first victory.

CHARLIE VITCHERS

In most people's minds, there were three "last days" that were going to be nationally recognized and remembered.

On May 28 was the ceremony the construction workers did for ourselves, the last column cut-down ceremony. We were actually ready to go earlier than that—and we needed to get that last column out of there to finish the job—but because some of the DDC administrators were going on a two- or three-week sailing trip from the Bahamas to Cancún or something, they told us we couldn't have our ceremony until they got back. They were pretty adamant, so we bumped it to the twenty-eighth.

The next ceremony was the last truck ceremony, when they carried the last column out by truck on May 30. The city put that party together.

We knew it really wasn't the last truck out. There was no way the last truck of debris was leaving this site on May 30, no way. The pit was clear but we knew we had another month to go because we had just gotten permission to look through 90 West and 130 Liberty for remains.

The real last truck ceremony didn't take place until June 25. That's when we took the last truckload of debris out of 130 Liberty Street, which was then turned over to its owner. But there were only a few of us still working by then.

The last column that the city used in their ceremony was the same one that we used in ours; it came from under the Tully Road, inside the southeast corner of the core of Tower Two. It was a heavy box beam, thirty-six feet tall, about four feet wide and two feet thick.

We were digging out Tully Road, and I was doing a walk

through with Lou Mendes. As we turned around, the top few feet of this column was sticking up out of the debris. It said "SQ 41" on it. Lou Mendes looked at me and he goes, "What the fuck is that?"

I said, "Well, that's the Squad 41 guys, they're looking for their buddies."

A supervisor from Tully, Brian Lyons, had a brother, Michael, who was in that squad, and I think a fireman named Eddie Walsh made the notation on that column. The fire department had lost a lot of guys in that area so he wrote "SQ 41" on the column so they knew to look there.

MICHAEL BANKER, FDNY

When it started out it wasn't even a column sticking up; the top was just a step off the ground. The label was for a specific fire company looking for their guys, and they were very dedicated.

When we started dismantling the road, this column was sticking up a couple of feet and used as a reference point for recoveries.

CHARLIE VITCHERS

The city was already planning their last truck ceremony and had asked for a piece of steel to put on a truck. Lou said to me, "Why don't we make that the last column?"

I looked at him and said, "Yeah, why not? Let's put a flag on it then so the ironworkers don't burn it down." I went to the 5:30 meeting and announced to the guys that that was going to be the last column and I wanted somebody to go out there and put a flag on it. The ironworkers went out and welded a flag pole onto that beam and stuck a flag on it.

At the time, there was no plan to make the cut-down of that column a big ceremony. We—the construction workers—hadn't planned any ceremony. But now that we had this column of significance the word got out that that was going to be the last column. Now, all of a sudden, as we excavated around the column, people came to write their name or put their pictures of their loved ones on there or claim that spot for their own agency.

Squad 41 never had any intention of that. To them that beam meant that their guys were in that area. That beam had no other significance. But then the cops had to put on "PAPD 37," for the thirty-seven members they lost, then the NYPD put "NYPD 23," the fire department put "FDNY 343," and a carpenter put up "2,762," the number of civilians lost.

MICHAEL BANKER, FDNY

As the levels went down, the column stayed and people started painting it and attaching pictures of some of the victims that were lost.

Someone taped my close friend Dennis Cross's picture on the column right at the B-6 level. I called his wife from the site; she thought it was a great idea, an honor. I got some duct tape and made sure it stayed on.

WILLIE QUINLAN, IRONWORKER

The only way I can explain it is the last column was like a huge tombstone. The police and the firemen came down and put all their buddies' names and pictures on there and the families would come and visit the column. We had a flag on top of it and a lot of people signed it. Like I said, it was like a tombstone.

CHARLIE VITCHERS

As the debris around the column came down, it became more and more important that the column didn't get destroyed. The question became, "How are we gonna get it down?" because now you can't just burn it and cut it, now we've got to handle it with kid gloves.

Originally, the construction workers wanted to do a last truck ceremony for the last truck of debris from the site, not a column. We wanted to have the last truck go up the ramp to the sound of a beating drum, a beat for every person who lost their life down there. We presented a plan to the city.

But the city shot us down. They said, "No, you can't do that because we're not shutting down the West Side Highway and we already have a planned ceremony, we just don't know what the date's going to be. We're going to have our own last truck removal ceremony." Then they told me no construction people would be allowed to partake in the last truck ceremony.

We said, "Well, piss on you, then." So we did the column ceremony instead.

•　　•　　•

On May 30, the city held a very public ceremony for the last official truck. It was a high-profile event attended by the DDC, the mayor's staff, the fire department, the police department, even the Department of Sanitation. Bloomberg was there. So was Giuliani, so was New York governor George Pataki. Hundreds of reporters covered the event. Construction workers, however, weren't invited. At least, not at first.

BOBBY GRAY

I was infuriated when we weren't invited to what was supposed to be the final ceremony. I was freaked out. I'm a die-hard union person—I believe in them, I think they're a good thing—and they didn't want to invite any of the men and women who worked on the site. Other than the victim's families, who I agreed should be there, it was going to be all the highfalutin' people, the politicians and people who probably never stepped foot in there.

CHARLIE VITCHERS

After they told us no construction workers could attend the last truck ceremony, I received a letter requesting that I attend a meeting about the logistics of the ceremony. At the meeting I said, "Listen, I'm speaking for the construction workers. You guys *cannot* leave out the construction workers from this last truck ceremony."

They offered to give me fifteen people. I said, "That's not enough."

So they asked, "Well, how many people do you want?"

I said, "I want two hundred and fifty," or something.

They say, "Charlie, you can have one hundred people in the site, but we want their names. And you can have fifteen people on the honor guard of the bridge, and I want their names, too, but I've got to have them by 2 P.M."

So we went back to the trailer. I told everyone, "We need one hundred and fifteen names. We're going to pick." I got all of the union's representatives, the captains and the foremen from each, and I had them all write down the names of all the people that they had working for them and I threw them all in Steve Rasweiler's fire hat, and I asked Steve to pick them because I wanted everybody to know it was being done fairly.

The first hundred we picked out were for those just allowed on-site. The last fifteen were the people on the honor guard. And the very last one picked would be allowed to help carry the gurney up the hill with the other agencies.

Pia Hofmann was the last name pulled out of the hat.

She wasn't in the room, and when we drew her name out of the hat, Bobby Gray just gave a big sigh, and Steve Rasweiler is like, "Oh, Pia."

Nobody knew what her reaction was going to be. She's got a great heart, great attitude, but she'll tell you exactly what she thinks. That's why she was able to stay down on the site for eight months, that's why she did what she did. But I was so happy.

PIA HOFMANN, OPERATING ENGINEER

To this day I still don't believe that. I don't care what anybody says. I think it was a setup. Bobby called me and told me. I kept asking him and he goes, "No, I swear to you. We put all these names in the hat and you were the last one to be picked." I'm like, "No, you're kidding, right?" He goes, "No."

I didn't buy it. I mean, here I was, the female Local 14 operator, I don't know . . . I don't have luck like that.

You know what an honor it was for me to do that?

CHARLIE VITCHERS

It meant a lot to her and the 114 other construction workers they allowed in. But 90 percent of the construction workers weren't even allowed to be there to watch. We weren't allowed past Chambers Street.

I had a pass. I could have gone anywhere. I could have sat on the governor's shoulder.

I chose not to. I went up to Chambers Street and hung out with the guys.

The job was not quite finished, though. Ninety West Street and 130 Liberty, which stood outside the site, had been sealed for months, marked for demolition. Vitchers felt strongly, however, that they still needed to be searched. A number of remains had been found in each building before they were sealed, and before he left he wanted to make sure, with his own eyes, there was nothing left to find.

CHARLIE VITCHERS

We were just making sure we didn't leave any stone unturned, because it was time to close up and give the job back to the Port Authority.

They had turned 90 West and 130 Liberty over to the owners too early. The city had told them, "We searched it."

That was ridiculous. They hadn't been fully searched, so we went back there in June for another three weeks searching them again. There were debris piles and gashes through those buildings. We took body parts off of the scaffolds and off of the roofs. It was terrible to find bones almost a year later.

We didn't want anybody to find a finger after we left. One thing Mike Banker said to me one day made me think.

"You know," he said, "how the old buildings in the city were built, one alongside of the other, with that little six-inch space? You can't get a man in there. Between 125 Cedar and 90 West Street, there's a four- to six-inch space between the buildings that goes for twenty-two stories."

He says, "I bet there's bones in there." Suppose there was somebody's skull in there, or somebody's arm or leg?

I said to him, "If you want us to knock the fucking building down, we will fucking knock the building down."

He goes, "Let me think about it."

Two days later we went up to the roof of 90 West Street with high-pressure fucking hoses and we blew out all the debris from in between those two buildings.

On June 25, we took the last load of searched debris out of 130 Liberty Street and got the final sign-off from the fire department—it was like a 30-yard container of debris.

Understand, I had been working with guys like Sam and Mike

and Steve Rasweiler. They were just firefighters, running the job, making decisions on behalf of the city. It was really weird because I wasn't dealing with the brass, but these common firemen, and I'm a common construction worker, and we were making major decisions. They just said, "Okay, we don't need to look here anymore," and I said, "Okay," and they signed off. But we only got to that point because we walked the site eighteen times or something and made sure. It was a good thing we did because we found stuff at the end and that's what kept the job going so long.

We did the right thing. There were only a handful of guys, maybe twenty-five, who really hung in there to the very end, because the job had dwindled down. Hauling out that last load of debris was the real end for us. That was it.

The next morning I came in with the same small crew. I had asked for the Port Authority to be there. It was their site now and we were turning it back over to them.

I went out to the store and bought three clean slate notebooks, nothing in them, and brought them to our 8 o'clock meeting. After the meeting, I made a little announcement that we were officially turning the site back over to the Port Authority. I handed Peter Rinaldi, Ed McGinley, who was another Port Authority engineer, and Lt. John Ryan of PAPD a notebook and told them, "We're giving you a clean slate. You accept it or we stay here."

And the three of them just shook my hand and said, "Charlie, you did a great job. We accept the job." That was it.

That's how we did things down there. We did with a handshake what you normally can't do without a letter of credit or money in the bank. In any other situation if I had to turn a job over to the Port Authority, it would have taken me another six months just to clean up the paperwork. On that job down there it was a handshake and an acknowledgment that we're turning over a completely safe job. It's been dug out; it's been cleaned; it's been signed off by the fire department; recovery has ended.

I said, "If there's any punch list for the job, let me have it now."

But there was no punch list. These guys just said, "Nope. Thank you very much."

All of a sudden, I had turned the site over and now other people were making the decisions. They even changed the badges.

It was funny. Later that day I went out for a beer with Peter Rinaldi and got a phone call while I was in the pub. Someone was saying that they had removed my pass out of the window of my car down at the site.

I'm like, "What are you talking about?"

Somebody had borrowed my pass because he wanted to get something out of his office and he didn't have a pass. But when I went back to get my car, I wasn't allowed on-site! Here I was with the head engineer of the Port Authority and I had been deleted from the computer! I wasn't even allowed back on-site to get my car! I went over to the security trailer, asked to see the guy that deleted me. The security guard said, "Oh, he just left, Charlie. I know who you are but I can't do it. I have orders from the Port Authority."

I started to laugh. "You son of a bitch."

It took about five minutes to track the guy down. I got reinstated and that was that. I'm sure they canceled me again the moment I left.

The ceremony that really mattered to the workers didn't happen on May 30, or even June 25. It took place on May 28. After nine months, the ceremony on that day was just for the construction workers.

CHARLIE VITCHERS

What we did was take the program we had designed for the last truck ceremony we had wanted to do and made it work for a last column ceremony. But we kept it in the pit, just for the construction workers. Then the fire department asked us if they could bow for the moment of silence.

We said, "Okay, we can use a bow for the moment of silence."

And then the Port Authority police said, "What can we do?"

I said, "Well, you guys can bring the flag down and help us drape the flag over the piece of steel."

Then I went to the fire department and the police department individually, not as any part of a formal meeting. I said, "Listen, guys, we're going to have our column cut-down ceremony on May 28. At the end of the ceremony you guys are going to be there, but I want you guys to leave first and to line up on the bridge and salute the construction workers as they leave." And Steve Rasweiler says, "WOW, that's a fucking great idea. You know, without you guys we wouldn't have gotten through it, I've got no problem with that."

John Ryan of PAPD says, "I got no problem with that."

By the middle of May it was Fleet Week and Captain Armstrong, from the USS *Iwo Jima,* and another officer wanted to know if they could help.

Terry Sullivan, a Bovis supervisor who was my right-hand man and who was setting up the program, said, "Captain Armstrong wants to meet us out in front of the Marriott hotel at West and Albany at noon. Let's go talk to him, because I've got 2,000 flags to give out to the construction workers after the event, but I don't have anybody to fold them. Maybe those guys will fold them."

So we met Armstrong and another officer and they asked, "How can we help you guys?"

Terry goes, "I got two thousand American flags, three by five, and we need to get them folded."

Armstrong says, "No problem. We'll get them out to the ship and we'll ask the guys to volunteer their time."

And then they asked, "What else?"

I said, "Do you have a couple of sailors that might want to come down and hang out on the ramp and salute the construction workers after the event?"

Captain Armstrong looks at me and he goes, "I don't know. A lot of these guys are on liberty, but I might get fifty guys to come down."

Well, I'll tell you what. The night of that thing, after that ceremony was done, the construction workers turned around, and there were 150 sailors on the bridge.

I also sent a letter to Mayor Bloomberg, inviting him down. I got a call back from his public relations representative. She goes, "He's accepted your offer to be down there. What do you want him to do?"

"If he could help hand out flags to the guys as they come up the bridge," I said, "that would be great."

All I wanted to do was get recognition for the construction workers who in a week or two were all going to be gone from the job. And I also wanted to invite back those people who had already left the site. I had special badges made up. They said "Last Column." We gave out 2,500 of them.

If it wasn't for that event, the construction workers would have felt cheated because we were being sent off the site without any recognition or any way to end the job.

Before the last column cut-down ceremony, the regular full trailer crew all sat around together for the last time. We still had fifty or sixty people on the job, and we held a regular meeting.

I had a sign-up sheet and I just told everybody, "This is it, this is our day." Whatever I said made them tear up. Then I just said, "I want to go around the table one at a time, whatever you have to say, whatever's on your mind, we're closing out, now's the time to talk. Get the group together because a lot of people are going to be leaving real soon." We went around the room and I asked everybody how they felt at this point in time.

We just had people break down, crying. Mike Banker from the fire department was in there. I think I started with him because he's this rough, tough, no-nonsense guy. You should have seen the guy. He broke down and cried like a baby. All he said was, "Hey, we were dead in the water without you guys."

You remember things like that.

Every single person in there had something to say about how the whole event affected them personally, emotionally, physically, whatever. You saw some pretty big guys in there just break down, just cry their eyes out. It was unbelievable. They needed it because they knew the job was over. That meeting took about four hours. You want to talk about emotion . . .

Nobody knew how to say good-bye. We had guys that couldn't handle leaving. The ceremony was a collective psychotherapy thing. Everybody needed it. They needed something for themselves. It was like, "To hell with everybody else, we were doing it for ourselves." We didn't want any media, we didn't want anybody covering it.

The construction workers held their last column ceremony at the end of the work day beneath a gray-blue sky at twilight. The timing was important. Most of the construction workers were already at work on other jobs by now, and job sites don't stop for ceremonies—not even this one. There were no speeches, no celebrities, no VIPs, just the men and women who had done the work coming together to witness the end.

Before the ceremony began, many of the workers still assigned to the job gathered around the column. Its most obvious markings were the enormous stenciled numbers recognizing the uniformed and civilian dead. But as well, there were the numbers of the various union locals. A steady stream of men and women approached the lower end of the column and began to add their names and personal messages. Others took photographs, shot video, and—for the first time—scribbled down the phone numbers and addresses of people they'd worked with, side by side, for nearly nine months.

At 7 P.M., in hard hats, blue jeans, fluorescent orange safety vests, and work boots, they joined nearly 2,000 workers who were returning to the site one last time, at Vesey and West Street. Most had left the site months before; others, like Bobby Gray, Charlie Vitchers, and Willie Quinlan, would be back in the pit the following morning.

Some cried and others laughed. Many were seeing one another in street clothes for the first time, hair combed and fingernails clean. They fell in line behind a pipe and drum corps from the carpenter's union, Local 608, and slowly walked down West Street—not marching, just walking together.

As they reached the bridge and turned to walk down into the pit, they were greeted with a smattering of applause. But there were no huge crowds of New Yorkers, no satellite trucks, no throngs of reporters. Just their fellow workers from Ground Zero—cops and firemen—family members, and the sailors from the Iwo Jima.

Nearly nine months before, on September 11, 2001, many of these men and women had determinedly trudged against a steady stream of New Yorkers fleeing the site of one of America's greatest tragedies. Many of those same workers now walked into the pit for the last time. They did not rush, choosing instead to linger as if entering the site for the first time. Around the perimeter, safety nets hung from still-damaged buildings. The slurry wall towered naked above them. Apart from the last column, the slurry wall was the only structure on the site that had not fallen, or been torn down and hauled away. Still holding back the waters of the Hudson, the wall was a testament to their labor.

As the workers gathered together at the bottom of the pit, ironworkers burned through the iron flagpole welded onto the giant column.

Jim Abadie carried the flag to the small reviewing stand, joining Lou Mendes of the DDC, Charlie Vitchers, Willie Quinlan, and perhaps a dozen other workers. Quinlan and another ironworker folded the flag as a spontaneous chant of "USA" burst forth from the crowd.

A crane was maneuvered into position and hooked onto the column as the construction workers gathered around. Local 40 ironworkers, laborers from Local 79 and 731, dock builders from Local 1456, and Local 14 and 15 operating engineers passed a torch and cut loose the bracing. Then, ever so slowly, the crane lowered the column, gently, to horizontal.

As it descended, hands reached out to touch. Small clouds of concrete dust spilled off the top. No one spoke. The only sound was the backup beacon from the crane.

As the pipe and drum corps began to play "Amazing Grace," the crowd parted and a large tractor trailer backed into position, its bed draped with an enormous black cloth. Ironworkers adjusted the rigging, and the column was lowered into place.

Applause broke out once again. Pulling the black shroud over the column, workers strapped it into place and carefully draped an American flag on top.

Under a deepening twilight, saluted by the soldiers and sailors of the Iwo Jima, the firemen, and the cops with whom they had worked side by side for nine long months, the construction workers filed slowly out. At the top of the ramp, as promised, Mayor Bloomberg helped hand out flags.

In the distance, a bell tolled.

And then it was over.

BOBBY GRAY

It turned out to be way better than anything the city could have done for us. Even though I was very impressed with what the city pulled off two days later, our last column ceremony was much more meaningful.

At one point I looked up and the place looked like it was lined with sailors. I don't remember how they got there, but all of a sudden you just turned around and they were everywhere.

I was in tears towards the end, walking up the ramp. I had lost it at that point.

CHARLIE VITCHERS

Taking that column down was the last hurrah for most of the construction workers. That was it. We were celebrating the end. We were ready to leave.

EPILOGUE

The pit was empty. The massive slurry wall sat exposed, standing sentry over a vast gravesite. The last Superintendents Daily Report filed by Bovis, dated June 30, 2002, ended simply "No work today; paperwork only." The clean-up cost $750 million and entailed 3 million man hours of labor; more than 110,000 truckloads of debris, weighing 3.6 billion pounds, had been hauled off-site.

Yet, the real cost was in human life. The September 11 attacks killed 2,749 people at Ground Zero–1,152 are still unidentified. Workers helped recover 19,964 separate human remains.

Nearly five years after September 11, Bobby Gray, Charlie Vitchers, and the others still consider the nine months they spent at Ground Zero the most precious and most painful time of their lives. It was the worst job they had ever worked, and the best one they'll ever have. They don't want to do it again. But if needed, they would go in an instant.

They have returned to the outside world, to eight-hour shifts and five-day work weeks. But the specter of their time at Ground Zero is never far away.

For some of the people who worked on the cleanup, the transition has been difficult. From 2002 to 2004, Mount Sinai Hospital evaluated the mental and physical health of thousands of workers and volunteers who spent significant time at Ground Zero. In a report issued in September of 2004, more than half reported having emotional troubles, ranging from anxiety, panic attacks, and depression to problems either at work or at home. Fifty-one percent met threshold criteria for further mental health evaluation, yet prior to the study, only 3 percent had sought assistance. Sixty percent of those evaluated exhibited what the report termed WTC-related respiratory symptoms—dry cough, shortness of breath, wheezing, sinusitis, and other maladies. Those affected merely were counseled after their evaluation to seek medical attention. Treatment was not included as part of the study.

"I talk to people from down there all the time," says Charlie Vitchers. "People are still suffering psychological effects of what went on. Many claim that people don't understand what it is we saw down there. I get a lot of phone calls. Men's wives call me up sometime, and say, 'Charlie, can you give my husband a call? I just don't like the mood he's been in lately.' If a guy doesn't want to talk about it to his wife, he wants to talk about it to somebody else. So they talk to me. I go out for a beer with the guy, and everything's cool. We reminisce and bullshit and everything's fine."

Bobby Gray believes that "the worst thing that happened while we were there was that the real world was not our reality. So at the end, when it was over, the only people you could talk to about it were those people who were there."

Yet those who worked at Ground Zero take strength knowing that they are part of a special brotherhood. They share that connection with one another and no one else. They depend on that and their work to go on.

After forty years in the ironworker's union Willie Quinlan is contemplating retirement, and, perhaps, a return to Newfoundland. He laughs and says, "I finally got my time in." After Ground Zero, he recalls, "It was strange going back to work because when you were at the Trade Center, even though you worked twelve hours a day, seven days a week, you never wanted to leave. You always wanted to go back. You couldn't get enough sleep because you kept thinking about the job. You had to go back.

"I didn't realize until I left the job how much we went through. You say to yourself, 'How did I do it?'

"When I went back to a regular job, working forty hours a week, it was a breeze. There was nothing to it. Every day felt like a half day's work."

Pia Hofmann is still most comfortable on a machine, doing the work, staying busy. She remembers, "When I first went back to work, I felt totally unproductive. If you give me a job where I don't have much to do or I have a lot of downtime I find myself being very depressed.

"A little while after I left the Trade Center they made me a Master Mechanic. Don't get me wrong. I was honored to be a female Master Mechanic. But they made a big mistake. I was losing my mind; it was the worst thing they could have done to me, because I had too much idle time.

"People said to me, 'Oh, you must appreciate this idle time because most of the time you go on these jobs, you bust your ass.'

"I said, 'Those are the jobs I want!'

"It's very hard now because all the time down there at the Trade Center you felt like you had a purpose. You did this wonderful thing and you were productive and now . . ."

Today, Pia is back on machines.

Jim Abadie is still an executive with Bovis Lend Lease. In 2004 he was named principal-in-charge of the firm's New York office. His days are full of meetings, setting schedules, and long-range planning. Even before the work at Ground Zero ended, he was transitioning back, attending to other jobs.

"When the thing finally ended and everybody had to leave, a

lot of guys just never left," he says. "Anybody who was down there was changed. I just hope that they were changed in a good way. I hope they can look back on their time at Ground Zero with pride and then move on."

Peter Rinaldi is still an engineer for Port Authority with the title of general manager, World Trade Center site. Before 9/11, his office, like those of so many other Port Authority employees, was in the Trade Center. On vacation on September 11, he returned to find his workplace gone and many of his colleagues dead or missing.

Today, his office is at the corner of Broadway and Liberty Street, barely one block from the site. His window overlooks Ground Zero. Rinaldi will not forget what happened, but he is able to look ahead, focusing on the work he loves.

Of his time at Ground Zero he says, "It was like nothing any of us had ever been involved in before and hopefully we won't be again. The feelings at the site, in terms of the people wanting to do the right thing, of being motivated and driven by the common feeling that this was an attack, that we lost some of our fellow citizens and friends, that we wanted to do *something*, was unique. Everyone worked together to make things happen. I know for some people it was almost, well, not sad that it was ending, but we were all so caught up in everything . . . when it was coming to an end, it was hard."

Richard Garlock is a structural engineer for LERA, and he has taught at Princeton University. "I can't say I cherished being at Ground Zero, and I can't say it was the greatest thing that ever happened to me," he says. "That's not what it was about. We weren't special—I can't emphasize that enough.

"But . . . it's hard to come up with the words. It was a duty and a privilege being there.

"There were no serious injuries down there during the cleanup, and that's really something. The engineers and others who were concerned about safety were working hard to make sure that was accomplished. We worked on that every day. Everyone was there with their A team and their game face. There was no screwing around.

"When it was over, I certainly made some changes. I don't go into the office and work fourteen hours a day like I used to. I now work at home a couple days a week. I have young kids and I spend as much time with them as possible. You can't take life and family for granted. That's what I took to heart when I left the Trade Center. I'm happy to be home and be a part of my kids' lives."

Immediately after he left Ground Zero, Bobby Gray and a friend took off on their Harleys and, with no destination in mind, eventually ended up in Montreal. But after only five days, he returned to New York.

"When I got back," he says, "Bovis asked me to be the Master Mechanic at the AOL building, which I took as a pretty big compliment. I was lucky. I went to a job where there were four or five of us from the Trade Center, and after a short while Charlie Vitchers was there, too. But there were a lot of people who spent nine months on-site and went to a job where nobody had been at Ground Zero. Nobody knew what they had been through. That situation had to have been really, really tough.

"When I got to AOL, I was so burned out. All of a sudden fatigue just set in. Every half hour I felt like I needed to take a nap.

"I know I was thinking about the Trade Center at first. The thing is, when you are around people who haven't been there, you get peppered with questions. I *hate it* when that happens. I just give them a very short answer, very abrupt. Hopefully they catch the hint that I don't want to talk about it.

"Eventually I just buried myself in the work and let that be my exit strategy. The good thing was that the AOL job was a monster.

At the height of that job I had forty operating engineers working, which is unheard of. I had to accommodate different contractors calling for different types of jobs and get people in and get people out and go to all the meetings.

"I was very content doing what I was doing before September 11. I loved it. But as a Master Mechanic on a huge site, the phone is ringing at 8 o'clock at night and 5 o'clock in the morning!

"What sustains me is the thought that I can always go back and do what I did before, just run a crane. I could go back tomorrow and put my name out and have a good job running a tower crane.

"I like putting on my boots and my work clothes. I like the feeling I get climbing on a piece of steel and being up high. I always want to be able to do that."

In 2004, Gray and Jo-Ann Farley bought a house together in Yorktown Heights, New York, where they live with her two daughters. Gray doesn't worry about himself, but his concern over the men and women he worked with is never very far away.

"If there are ill effects later on," he says now, "I think it's probably going to be most damaging mentally and emotionally. As a group, construction workers don't really communicate. I've never been a great communicator. I just do my job.

"But I feel pretty confident, pretty good. I look at what could have been and what other people have gone through and in the end I'd rather take my problems and be happy. I feel like I've come to accept what we saw and what we did. Has it affected me, has it changed me? Yeah. But compared to most I got off relatively unscathed. I'm still glad I was there. I'm still glad I was a part of it. And if it happened tomorrow, I'd go back and try and help again.

"My ultimate wish would be to take every American by the hand and be able to walk them through what we saw down there. I mean, if you had a chance to stand on a hilltop and look down on Pearl Harbor, would you? I think most people would say yes. I would like to be able to take everybody to the Trade Center for just ten minutes and let them see what it really was like.

"It was not the way it looked on TV. On TV it was so far away. But when you were there, there were just a million things happening. There was a vibration, a physical hum, almost an emotional hum to the job.

"One night, months after the attacks, the Marriott reopened south of the site. I spent a night down there with one of my best friends from childhood. Before that, I hadn't had a chance to spend any time looking at the site from above. But up there, we had a pretty good view.

"I couldn't sleep. I kept looking out the window. And there was still a hum, a physical hum to the job site. That whole night, I'd lie down then I'd get back up and go look out the window and feel it."

Charlie Vitchers has gone on. In July 2002, just a few weeks after leaving Ground Zero, Vitchers and his girlfriend, Holly, traveled to Australia to visit friends. He recalls, "I fished the Great Lake of Tasmania and we camped in the Outback. It was great to get away."

When he returned to Bovis, his first assignment was at the American Museum of Natural History, just filling in for a few weeks. The transition back into the outside world was abrupt.

"It was weird," he remembers. "After working at the Trade Center, all of a sudden I was walking around the Hall of Oceans, fixing the whale. Guys weren't expecting me to be 100 percent and that felt weird—I felt like I was 100 percent. But people gave me the time to get back into building a real job. It took me a while to calm down."

By the fall, he had a full assignment again, working as a supervisor on the enormous AOL complex. Bobby Gray was there, and so were others from Ground Zero. Day by day, the routine of his regular life returned. On December 28, 2002, Charlie Vitchers and Holly were married.

On the weekends, Charlie Vitchers can be found fishing on his boat in the middle of the lake near his home in Pennsylvania. During the week, Vitchers still works for Bovis as a general superintendent. In October 2005, he was assigned to a new job—a supervisor overseeing the demolition of 130 Liberty Street.

Nearly five years after September 11, 2001, Charlie Vitchers will be back at Ground Zero.

Those who didn't work at Ground Zero remain curious about the job. Just as construction workers once peppered those who built the Trade Center with questions, now they ask Charlie Vitchers about his nine months at Ground Zero. Twenty years from now, forty years from now, the job will still be talked about. The cleanup of the Trade Center—not its construction—now stands as the touchstone for New York's construction industry.

For Charlie Vitchers, Bobby Gray, and the thousands of other construction workers who spent time at Ground Zero, it is never very far away. It never will be.

CHARLIE VITCHERS

The people who died down there were from every culture in the world. Could you tell who was black and who was white when you removed the body? Absolutely not. It didn't matter.

On this site it didn't matter who you were. You were a burner, you were an ironworker, you were an operator, an engineer, a cop, a fireman. Whatever you were down there, you were working. You were doing your twelve-hour shift. You were not stopping. You were putting out your own heart, just to get this job done.

This was special all the way through. For the people I worked with, it was definitely special all the way through. Most people were there for the cause, to do the right thing.

There was never a time for me when it started to feel like just another job.

Among the people who worked down at the Trade Center, and even among construction people who didn't work down there, there's a conversation about 9/11 every day. I'm with a crew now and none of them worked down there except the general super, who lasted a day, and another guy who was down there for one eight-hour shift. He couldn't go back. But we all talk about it. We sit around and bullshit and converse about it every day.

It's important to a lot of people to be able to say we played a part down there, whatever it was. A lot of people take a lot of pride in the fact that they were down there and did what they did.

It's like a badge of honor. It was a very tough role and I think a lot of men and women today feel that they will never again have the opportunity they had at Ground Zero. It meant a lot to us, personally, and I think it really meant a lot to the nation.

The construction workers like myself who went down there, we're not an organization that's usually recognized by anybody. We were just a bunch of people who went in there and did what we had to do.

Now we're "just" ironworkers again and "just" carpenters again. We're working from blueprints and working from a schedule and a budget.

It was a whole different world, but we'll never forget it.

ACKNOWLEDGMENTS

Charlie Vitchers, Bobby Gray, and everyone who chose to participate in this project did so with the hope that their words would, in some way, represent the thoughts and feelings of all those who worked with them at Ground Zero. In that spirit, the authors would like to extend their thanks to the entire construction industry and every contractor, trade union, tradesman, agency, volunteer, and others who gave of themselves and spent time at Ground Zero, the Pentagon, and the crash site of Flight 93 in Shanksville, Pennsylvania. It is our hope that this book brings honor to their achievements.

Neither Charlie Vitchers nor Bobby Gray are profiting from this project. At their insistence, their share of the proceeds have been designated for charity.

This book was created from more than seventy hours of transcribed taped interviews with Charlie Vitchers, Bobby Gray, and the others quoted in the text, supplemented by a wide variety of print resources, documents, journals, photographs, videos, and other material. Everyone interviewed was offered the opportunity to check their statements for accuracy, and we thank them for their cooperation and participation. In addition, a number of people were interviewed whose comments were not included in the book. These participants range from other workers, local residents, volunteers, and members of the various agencies assigned to Ground

ACKNOWLEDGMENTS

Zero. Their contributions were no less valuable in the creation of this portrait.

Stephanie Peters, Robin Slater, and, most notably, Debbi Bradley worked diligently and patiently transcribing hours and hours of taped interviews under tight deadlines. Without their efforts, this project would not have been possible. Max Frazee—close friend, colleague, construction worker, and artist—brought the authors together and without his effort and input it is unlikely this book would ever have been written.

Our families all gave of themselves to allow us to complete this project, and we extend our thanks and love to them, particularly Holly Vitchers, Jo-Ann Farley, her daughters Mikela and Dylan, and Siobhan and Saorla Stout. Joel Meyerowitz generously allowed us access to his remarkable photographic archive, and his assistants, Ember Rilleau and Jon Smith, graciously responded to our queries. Agent John Taylor "Ike" Williams and his assistant Hope Denekamp of the Kneerim-Williams Agency at Fish and Richardson believed in this book from the start and backed us up the entire way. We also thank Katie Hall for her suggestions, editor Nan Graham, Anna deVries, John Fulbrook, and everyone else at Scribner for allowing us the opportunity to publish this project.

TIMELINE

September 11, 2001

8:46 A.M.: American Airlines Flight 11 slams into the North Tower.

9:03 A.M.: United Airlines Flight 175 strikes the South Tower.

9:50 A.M.: South Tower collapses.

10:29 A.M.: North Tower collapses

5:20 P.M.: Building Seven collapses.

Bobby Gray, Charlie Vitchers, and Jim Abadie arrive on-site. Michael Banker and Sam Melisi arrive on-site at various times during the course of the day.

September 12, 2001

New York City Department of Design and Construction, the DDC, divides the site into four quadrants, each managed by a different construction company. The last survivor is pulled from the pile. Ironworker Willie Quinlan arrives on-site.

September 13, 2001

Under the direction of the DDC, a team of more than thirty structural engineers begins to inspect the structural integrity of buildings on the periphery of the site.

September 16, 2001

Workers clear enough debris from West Street on the west side of the site to allow for construction traffic.

September 17, 2001

Volunteers begin to be removed from the site as authorized construction workers, fire and police personnel, and emergency services workers take over search and recovery activities.

September 19, 2001

Construction trailers are wired with electricity to generators. Pia Hofmann arrives on-site.

September 21, 2001

Following dredging operations at Pier 25 and Pier 6, Weeks Marine begins removing debris by barge from Pier 6 to Fresh Kills Landfill in Staten Island. Previously, all debris had been transported by truck. The barge operation from Pier 25 begins a few days later.

September 22, 2001

Bovis receives delivery of a standard, 50-foot construction trailer to serve as their site headquarters.

September 24, 2001

Press reports identify the potential collapse of the slurry wall as an issue. Mayor Giuliani announces that many victims will likely never be recovered and that it is unlikely that survivors will be found. Operations transform from a rescue operation to a recovery operation.

September 25, 2001

The first of three attempts is made to pull down the façade of the South Tower with grapplers.

September 26, 2001

Charlie Vitchers learns he will be assigned to Ground Zero indefinitely as a general superintendent on the day shift.

September 28, 2001

More than 134 tons of debris have already been removed and officials begin to realize the cleanup may not take as long as their initial assessment indicated. Mayor Giuliani announces that the cleanup will take "anywhere from nine months to a year." Three hundred and six bodies have been recovered. The official number of missing people is downgraded to 5,960.

October 3, 2001

To relieve water pressure on the slurry wall, wells are installed outside the perimeter to remove groundwater.

October 7, 2001

Cut-down of South Tower façade begins. United States begins bombing raids in Afghanistan.

October 8, 2001

Earth-pressure-wedge crack discovered outside the slurry wall on Liberty Street. Over the next week more than 50,000 yards of fill is dumped on the inside of the slurry wall to hold it in place.

October 12, 2001

Workers begin to remove debris to allow the tieback operation to reinforce the slurry wall along Liberty Street.

October 13, 2001

So-called Tully Road, a pathway of compressed debris on the southern edge of the site, is complete. Grapplers, trucks, and other heavy equipment can now get into the pile to remove debris. Recovery operations beneath the road are suspended. More than 290,000 tons of debris have been removed and more than 1,300 construction workers are on-site.

October 17, 2001

First slurry wall tiebacks are installed.

October 22, 2001

The final portion of the façade of the South Tower, the west wall, is cut down.

October 30, 2001

Citing safety concerns, Mayor Giuliani announces plans to scale back the number of FDNY on-site from approximately 160 to 25, and the number of NYPD and PAPD police officers from 90 to 25.

October 31, 2001

Cache of gold and silver worth at least $200 million is removed from the vault of the Bank of Nova Scotia beneath Building Four.

November 1, 2001

The DDC proposes covering the site with a giant tent to shelter workers from the elements. The impractical plan is quickly abandoned.

November 2, 2001

Firefighters protest city plans to scale back their presence on-site, resulting in a brief scuffle with police. The city backs down and eventually allows seventy-five firefighters to remain on-site.

November 6, 2001

Michael Bloomberg is elected mayor of New York City.

November 20, 2001

Demolition of Building Five by wrecking ball begins. A few days earlier, Building Four was demolished by the same method.

November 22, 2001

Official number of missing is dropped to fewer than 3,400.

December 2, 2001

Antenna that sat atop the North Tower is located.

December 17, 2001

Last portion of the façade of the North Tower, known as the shrouds on the northeast corner, is taken down. Attempt to pull down Building Six begins. Truck ramp reaches B-6 level.

December 18, 2001

Large portion of Building Six is pulled down. The remainder is taken down in a controlled demolition.

December 19, 2001

One hundred days after the attack, New York governor George Pataki announces that the fires burning beneath the pile have been extinguished. That blaze represented the longest commercial building fire in American history.

December 30, 2001

Public viewing platform overlooking the site opens on Church Street.

January 1, 2002

2,340 victims remain missing or unidentified.

January 7, 2002

Bovis Lend Lease officially takes over as sole point of contact for cleanup activities, effectively placing the cleanup under their authority as designated by the DDC.

January 31, 2002

Tully Construction Company awarded contract to rebuild the PATH and subway station on-site and repair tunnels.

February 11, 2002

Two World Financial Center reopens.

February 20, 2002

Damaged PATH train cars removed.

March 1, 2002

At a cost of $2.5 million, the 515-foot-long Acrow prefabricated bridge, weighing 350 tons, is completed. Removal of Tully Road and search for victims beneath the road begins.

March 11, 2002

Reconstruction of West Street for public use begins. The Tribute in Light memorial is installed and is on display each evening through April 14.

May 10, 2002

1,072 victims have been identified. Another 1,796 remain missing. 19,435 body parts have been recovered. 1.4 million tons of debris have been removed.

May 28, 2002

Last column cut-down ceremony for construction workers takes place, marking the cut-down of column 1001B from the South Tower.

May 30, 2002

Last truck ceremony takes place, marking the removal of the last column from the site.

June 25, 2002

Final truck ceremony. The cleanup officially ends, although some workers remain on-site shoring up the remnants of Building Six around the PATH tube's northern projection, and work on the PATH and subway lines continues. Charlie Vitchers turns the site over to Port Authority officials.

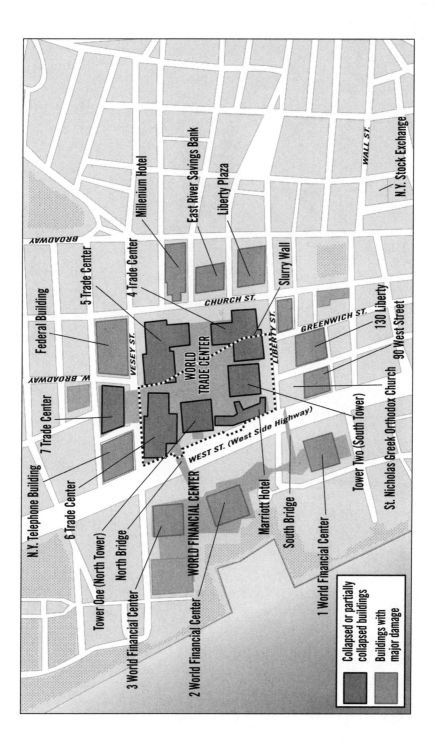

ABOUT THE AUTHORS

GLENN STOUT has served as series editor of *The Best American Sports Writing* since its inception and has published articles in many national and regional publications. He worked his way through Bard College in the construction industry as a concrete laborer and form carpenter. He lives in Vermont.

CHARLIE VITCHERS has worked in all aspects of the construction industry for more than thirty years. A native of Manhattan, Vitchers served as a general superintendent at Ground Zero. He is a general superintendent for Bovis Lend Lease and recently completed work on the new Time Warner Center building. An avid fisherman and outdoorsman, he lives in Pennsylvania and New York City.

BOBBY GRAY has been a member of the International Union of Operating Engineers for more than twenty-five years. Raised in Yonkers, Gray served as the Master Mechanic at Ground Zero. He also worked on the Time Warner Center building. When he's not working, Gray races automobiles and travels extensively. He lives in New York.